# JESUS APPRENTICE

## A MOVEMENT OF TAX
## COLLECTORS & FISHERMEN

40 one day readings

## Wes Davis

JESUS APPRENTICE

# Author's Note

This book is about a journey. You are invited to go on a mission with Jesus to help heal the world.

This mission began long ago when humans first chose to rebel—to make themselves the center of the story—rather than their Creator. That original sin resulted in breathtaking brokenness in our world that results with all of us being born with a self-centered nature that separates us from God. Since that original rebellion God has been at work to win back our hearts and take us with him in putting the world right again.

What if you went on that mission? What if you gave your life to the mission like the first apprentices of Jesus did? What would change in your world? What would change in you? Do you want to find out?

This book has 40 one day readings – five readings per week for eight weeks. A *Big Idea*, *Question*, and *Think about Jesus' words* are included at the end of each reading.

The book is written in second person using present tense verbs wherever possible to help you experience the mission like one of Jesus' twelve original apprentices. It's also a reminder that this mission is still going on today, and Jesus is at work inviting you to join him.

Finally, *Jesus Apprentice* is not an individual study-- just as Jesus didn't teach His apprentices in isolation. Take the journey together with other people – a small group of apprentices – because no one does the mission alone. Not even Jesus.

I would love to hear what Jesus is doing in your life and in those around you as you go on this mission with him. Tell me your stories!  Here is my phone number: 360-689-3444.

## On the mission with Jesus,
## Wes

## What does it mean to follow Jesus?

*… Anyone who intends to come with me has to let me lead. You're not in the driver's seat; I am. Don't run from suffering; embrace it. follow me and I'll show you how. Self-help is no help at all. Self-sacrifice is the way, my way, to finding yourself, your true self. Matthew 16:24 (Message)*

# CONTENTS

## Week One
# Jesus wants to
# heal the world

### Jesus came to change the world

*God didn't go to all the trouble of sending his Son merely to point an accusing finger, telling the world how bad it was. He came to help, to put the world right again.*
*John 3:17 (Message)*

# Introduction
## Week One

Every day you see things in the world that you think should be different. So does God.

Do you see the huge problems of the world and wonder if God is real? Do you see the huge problems of the world and wonder how human beings can be so cruel? What are you going to do about the problems of the world? They seem so big.

God sent Jesus into the world to put the world right again. Jesus is on a mission to heal this world by changing people's hearts, starting with twelve apprentices.

If Jesus came today and called you to be one of his twelve apprentices, would you go? What would change if you did? If you don't, you'll never know. If you do, the world will never be the same.

Jesus wants to heal the world.

## Day 1
# The world needs help.

### Jesus' heart breaks for the world

*When he saw the crowds, he had compassion on them because they were confused and helpless, like sheep without a shepherd. He said to his disciples, "The harvest is great, but the workers are few." Matthew 9:36-37 (NLT)*

**The world needs help.** I'm sure you agree. So, what are you going to do about it? "What do you mean – what am I going to do about it?" you ask. "Isn't that God's job? Where's God? What's _he_ going to do about it?"

Two great questions: "Where's God?" and "What's he going to do about it?" These are the same two questions that people were asking when Jesus came into the world.

Okay…now let's say you were born around the same time as Jesus. And like him, you are a Jew living 2,000 years ago during the days of the Roman Empire. How would you think about the world? What would your dreams be?

If you were brought up like most of the Jewish people, you would be dreaming of the day that the Messiah would come. Why? Because he would change your world.

In your mind, the Messiah (or Christ), would be a Warrior-King (Son of the Warrior-King David), and would change your world by defeating the Romans. Then, you would be able to live freely in your own kingdom with your own king. And finally, you and your people would be happy.

However, some of your people (perhaps even you) had given up the dream of freedom and lost faith in God. Almost 600 years now had passed since your people were conquered and scattered around the world. Where was your God then and where is he now?

Your religious leaders told you that this was God's judgment on your people for not living up to the standard of the Law given to you by one of your founding fathers, Moses. In fact, your leaders would write more rules (like 600 more) that would clearly explain how you could better keep the Law (10 commandments) so that God would be pleased.

From this, two very different worlds emerged that you could call the Kingdom of Religion and the Kingdom of Rome.

People in the Kingdom of Religion believed: "If everyone could keep the Law for one day, then the Messiah would come." They thought that the reason there are huge problems in the world is because people are bad. And bad people need religious rules to become better people.

People in the Kingdom of Rome thought: "This is pointless – all these silly rules; why not live like the Romans live and enjoy life? They thought that if everyone would simply embrace the rule of Rome (Pax Romana-Roman Peace), then people would be free from religion to find personal happiness.

If you were one of the people who rejected the teaching of the religious leaders, you were labeled "immoral." If you rejected the Roman way of life, you were labeled "foolish" or "backwards."

So…which world would you choose - pursuing the Roman peace and the pleasures it promised or religiously keeping rules?

Jesus chose neither.

Jesus saw the huge problems in the world and knew they could not be solved by "the Kingdom of Rome" or "the Kingdom of Religion."

He brought a new way of living called "The Kingdom of God" – a Kingdom that changes the world by changing people's hearts.

Jesus came to put the world right again, and at the age of 30, Jesus went public with his mission.

It wasn't long before word got out. Crowds of people who needed help came to him.

*"When he saw the crowds, he had compassion on them because they were confused and helpless, like sheep without a shepherd." (Matthew 9:36 NLT).*

Jesus saw the crowds and his heart broke. One person after another came to Jesus with emotional, relational, and physical needs. All of them with broken hearts.

Jesus asked – "Where are the workers?" Where is everyone who wants to help heal the world? Who cares about these people? Then he said to his disciples, *"The harvest is great but the workers are few. (Matthew 9:37 NLT)"*

Can you imagine living in a world in which huge problems exist and yet people argue over whether we're religious enough? That could never happen today, right?

Can you imagine living in a world with huge problems and yet people live for their own personal pleasure? We care too much to do that, don't we?

Is it possible that in our world of huge problems, two Kingdoms still exist? Isn't it true that there are still religious people trying to make you better and pleasure seekers trying to make you happy?

Which "kingdom" are you living in? Which "kingdom" do you want to live in? If your answer is neither, then keep reading. In this book you will learn a new way of living and get to be one of Jesus' apprentices on a mission to help heal the world. Because if you haven't noticed, the world needs help.

## The Big Idea:
The World needs help

## Question:
If you could change something in the world,
what would be different?

## Think about Jesus' words
*When he looked out over the crowds, his heart broke. So
confused and aimless, they were like sheep with no shepherd.*
*Matthew 9:36 (Message)*

# The World needs help now

**Jesus thinks the world needs changing now.**
*Jesus said, "No procrastination. No backward looks. You can't put God's kingdom off till tomorrow. Seize the day."*
Luke 9:62 (Message)

**The world needs help now.** The problems of the world simply will not wait. Now if you're like me, you believe that the world needs changing but you're not exactly sure where to start. Which Kingdom do you sign up for?

Should you jump on the Pax Romana boat and try to spread the best human government and way of living so people can have everything this world can offer? Or do you join the R.A.F. (Religious Armed Forces) and go to battle to try to make people better? Or maybe just complain about both?

Then one day, this Jesus that you've been hearing about comes your way. You're at work – maybe you're discussing the latest in Roman politics or perhaps the winner in last night's gladiator games – and Jesus walks into your life.

Right off, you like him. You like the fact that he doesn't put up with all that religious "stuff". You're intrigued that he seems so spiritual and yet so real. And you like the fact that he seems to really like you. In fact, he's the one that starts the conversation.

Over the course of your chit-chat, Jesus seems to be saying all of the things that your heart feels are right but have not been able to put into words. You find yourself saying, "Yeah...yeah...me, too."

Then he tells you about his mission to change the world. And while you're not exactly sure what he's talking about, you really like him...in fact, you kind of believe in him. "If anyone can change the world, he can."

One of the things he keeps talking about is this thing called the Kingdom of God and how the only way to change the world is to change people's hearts.

Then he says, "Follow me." And with that – you've been invited to go on this mission with Jesus to change the world.

Immediately you experience this rush of adrenaline. Wow...he's choosing me. Of all the people in the world...Jesus chooses me.

Then it hits you...me? Not me! You're flooded with all the reminders that you're not good enough and how Jesus would be making the biggest mistake of his life taking you with him.

Change the world by changing hearts...you can't do that – your heart needs changing, too.

Not wanting to offend him, you ask for a little bit of time to think about it. This is a big decision you tell him. There are a lot of things that you need to do to free yourself up to go on a mission like this. You will need to tell him tomorrow. He should understand that.
But he doesn't bite. Jesus looks right through your excuses and says, "No procrastination. No backward looks. You can't put God's kingdom off till tomorrow. Seize the day."

(Luke 9:62 Message)

Jesus stands in front of you. Time stands still. There you stand, trembling – heart racing. The decision you make in the next moment will change the rest of your life. What do you do?

There's a lump in your throat…you swallow…still undecided.

Jesus turns. He walks toward the door. It opens, he passes through and the door begins to close. Then something from deep inside of you – a hunger that causes you to lunge forward and slip through the door just before it shuts.

You follow.

It's at that moment that you discover the mission of bringing God's Kingdom to solve the huge problems of the world starts with a change in your own heart.

## The Big Idea:
The World needs help now

## Question:
What are you doing that is more important than changing the word?

## Think about Jesus' words
*You can't put God's Kingdom off until tomorrow. Seize the day. Luke 9:62 (Message)*

## Day 3
# You can't change the world alone

### Jesus chooses his twelve apprentices
*When Jesus saw his ministry drawing huge crowds, he climbed a hillside. Those who were apprentice to him, the committed, climbed with him. Arriving at a quiet place, he sat down and taught his climbing companions.*
*Matthew 5:1-2 (Message)*

**You can't change the world alone.** The problems of the world are bigger than you are.

These are the thoughts that are going through your head as you lay awake the next morning. What did you just sign up for? You told Jesus that you were going to leave your life and go on a mission with him to change the world. What on earth have you gotten yourself into now?

You get up. In a few hours, you will be meeting Jesus at the lake. As you're getting dressed, you think about how you're going to explain this to everyone in your life. Once ready, you walk out the door not knowing if or when you'll return.

As you get closer to the lake, traffic begins to slow down. Where is everyone headed? It appears that they are going to the same place you are. It looks like there are thousands all meeting Jesus at the lake.

This is a bit of let-down. Obviously, you weren't the only one Jesus invited.

You notice quite a mix of people – wearing everything from tattoos to designer togas, dreadlocks to mohawks, with bumper stickers pushing the latest slogans from the Kingdom of Rome and the Kingdom of Religion.

At the lake, Jesus makes his appearance. The crowd is so large that Jesus begins to hike up the mountain so everyone can see and hear him.

The crowd isn't sure what to do. Some of them immediately begin heading up the hill with Jesus, while others see this as their moment to slip away.

The thought crosses your mind – maybe this is your chance to change your mind. I mean, how would Jesus know if you left? There are plenty of people here to go on this mission and really, how much do you matter. If you leave now, you'll beat the traffic.

You start to leave, but then you think – if you leave now, what will you be missing? The adventure…you will definitely miss out on the journey. The mission…you will miss out on a chance to change the world. Jesus…you will miss out on the feeling you had yesterday when you were talking to Jesus.

The crowd thins between those who are climbing up to hear Jesus and those who are headed home. What do you choose? Are you going to go with these people or not?

Jesus looks back down the hill. He catches your eye. At this point you know you cannot go back. As you walk up the hill, you realize that you are going on the journey of a lifetime. You look around at the committed that are climbing with you.

You can't change the world alone. And you don't have to. Today, you have become part of a movement of people committed to help heal the world together with Jesus.

You know you believe in Jesus. You know that Jesus believes in you. You know that your life will never be the same again. You know that the only way to change the world is to change people's hearts. The only thing you still don't know is...what's going to happen next.

*Arriving at a quiet place, he sat down and taught his climbing companions. (Matthew 5:1-2 Message)*

## The Big Idea:
You can't change the world alone.

## Question:
What are you doing that is more important than changing the world?

## Think about Jesus' words
*Those who were apprentice to him, the committed, climbed with him. Matthew 5:1 (Message)*

# Day 4
# Jesus wants to
# change the world

## Jesus Heals a Leper

*Then a leper appeared and went to his knees before Jesus, praying, "Master, if you want to, you can heal my body." Jesus reached out and touched him, saying, "I want to. Be clean."*
*Matthew 8:2 (Message)*

**Jesus wants to change the world.** It is very obvious from what he just taught on the hillside that this Kingdom of God could really change people. You are amazed at his teaching and so are the other apprentices around you.

As Jesus walks back down the mountainside, you walk with some of the apprentices. There is a buzz. They tell you stories about some of the miracles that Jesus has already done in the surrounding towns and villages. People healed. Sickness gone. Disease gone. Evil spirits made to leave. The disabled walk. The blind see. Captives are freed. Families restored. Wow…you can't believe your ears and you wonder when you might be able to see some of these God-signs.

As Jesus gets to the bottom of the hill, there is a sea of people surrounding Him. You feel swallowed up as you and the others mix in with the crowd that stayed below. Everyone is curious to see what Jesus is going to do next.

Then, someone begins to move towards Jesus. You notice this because as the person nears Jesus there is an opening in the crowd. People jump out of the way to avoid coming in contact with this person. As he gets closer you can see his sores and smell his rotting flesh. He has leprosy.

You feel a mix of pity and fear – pity, because of his suffering – fear, because you don't want him touching you. He's unclean – religiously and physically unclean.

As you jump out of the way, you notice that Jesus moves towards him. Doesn't Jesus know that these open sores are contagious? Doesn't Jesus know that touching someone who is "unclean" will make him "unclean" too? Doesn't he know "unclean" people can't practice religion for a week? This could really hold the mission up! What is he thinking?

Just as the Leper reaches Jesus, he falls on his knees. "Master, if you want to, you can heal my body."

It is at this point you discover what the mission is about – it's about people – people who don't fit inside the religious rules and system. People who don't fit inside of your idea of what Jesus should do.

Jesus reaches out and touches the very person that the rest of us just avoided saying, "I want to. Be clean."

In some ways, you feel like Jesus isn't just speaking to the Leper – He's talking to you, too. "Be clean."

The Leper stands up completely healed. And so do you. And now, the mission to change the world by changing people's hearts has begun in both of you.

You realize that the mission is for the outsiders…the unclean…for all of us who feel sometimes like we want to connect with God but aren't sure if we're good enough. The unclean…all of us.

Jesus changes the world by changing people's hearts. And he isn't looking for twelve insiders who think they are already "clean" to go change the world. They won't be able to because their hearts won't change.

Jesus wants apprentices who know they need to change. He looks for people who are willing to do whatever it takes to get to him.

## The Big Idea:
Jesus wants to change the world.

## Question:
What does Jesus think needs changing?

## Think about Jesus' words
*Jesus reached out his hand and touched the man. "I am willing," he said. "Be clean!" Matthew 8:2 (Message)*

## Day 5

# If Jesus could choose an apprentice, he would choose you

### Jesus chooses Matthew to be an apprentice

*As Jesus was walking along, he saw a man named Matthew sitting at his tax collector's booth. "Follow me and be my disciple," Jesus said to him. So Matthew got up and followed him. Matthew 9:9 (NLT)*

If Jesus could choose an apprentice, he would choose you. And that is exactly what He did. As you follow Jesus, you look around at the others who are following, too. It isn't long before you begin to wonder about Jesus' selection process. Why did Jesus choose them? What was he thinking? They're not exactly the type that you would want to use a first-round draft pick on. Yes, it is true that you were doubtful about Jesus' wisdom in picking you, but that was before everything changed. Who are these people?

From the initial observations you can tell that a number of you are quite different – different political beliefs – different financial backgrounds – different passions and occupations – with different experiences and education. But one of the things that all of you have in common is this: none of you are religious leaders.

Why would Jesus come into the world and not choose any

religious leaders to change it? Jesus chose people like you--
and people like Matthew.

Matthew is one of the apprentices in your group and
Matthew is a tax collector. And being a tax collector meant
that he was fairly well known in the community – and not
for the things you want to be known for.

Tax collectors were traitors in your mind. They were Jews
collecting tax money from Jews for the Romans. Every time
these tax collectors came to your door you felt like they were
charging you a little extra for their own pockets. And every
time they came to your door you were reminded that the
Messiah had not come and you were not free.

Having Matthew on the team isn't exactly a popular decision
with the rest of the apprentices but it's not like Jesus asked
for a vote.

Jesus simply saw Matthew sitting at the tax collector's
booth. *"Follow me and be my disciple," Jesus said to him. So
Matthew got up and followed him." (Matthew 9:9 NLT)*

This wasn't popular with the religious leaders either. In fact,
when it came time for the religious leaders to slander Jesus,
they passed the word around that Jesus spent time with tax
collectors and prostitutes. In the mind of the religious
leaders, there really wasn't much of a difference. Both were
selling themselves out to get money.

This doesn't stop Jesus though. And it doesn't stop
Matthew. That evening Matthew throws a dinner party and
invites you and Jesus to his house. And to your surprise
when you arrive, all of Matthew's tax collector friends are
there, too.

At first nobody knows quite what to say, but Jesus goes right over to Matthew and embraces him. Immediately, Matthew introduces Jesus to all his friends. They seem really excited to meet him. Then Jesus introduces all of them to you and your apprentice group.

Everyone seems so nice and you wonder why you had judged them. Jesus seems to be teaching you something else about the mission – he doesn't judge people by their reputation or their outward appearance. Jesus accepts these people just as they are. And somehow this opens them up to accepting Jesus for who he is…and they accept you.

The party is more fun than you've had in a long time and there are groups of people everywhere talking about the mission. You're a bit surprised that they are also interested in changing the world – they're not exactly the religious type. But, neither is Jesus.

So maybe that is why Jesus is eating with them. Jesus likes that they are already connected to the culture. All of you are like Matthew in that you are somehow connected to people who are not interested in obeying all the religious rules. And many of you are caught up in the "Kingdom of Rome."

But all of you are hungry for something real. You are not interested in showing up in the temple and then going back to your regular life without the world changing.

Jesus likes that these people are willing to leave everything to follow him just as you left everything to follow him. And if you could choose anyone to follow, you would choose Jesus. And if Jesus could choose an apprentice, he would choose you. He did.

Now that you are a Jesus apprentice, you will learn the 7 practices that Jesus lives and breathes with his apprentices on the mission. It is how you change. It is how the world changes.

The seven practices are as follows:
1. Jesus invites us into his Life.
2. Jesus shows us his world.
3. Jesus lives in the culture.
4. Jesus apprentices volunteer their life to serve the world.
5. Jesus asks for everything.
6. Jesus changes people from the inside out.
7. Jesus apprentices make more apprentices.

## The Big Idea:
If Jesus could choose an apprentice,
he would choose you.

## Question:
Who are you going to change the world with?

## Think about Jesus' words
*"Follow me and be my disciple," Jesus said to him. So Matthew got up and followed him."*
*Matthew 9:9 (NLT)*

**Week Two**

# Practice #1:
# Jesus invites you
# into his life.

## Jesus comes to bring life

*A thief is only there to kill and steal and destroy. I came so that they can have real and eternal life, more and better life than they ever dreamed of.*
*John 10:10 (Message)*

# Introduction to
# Week Two

You can't help heal the world without getting to know God. And that is exactly what God wants you to do. In fact, Jesus invites you to get to know God by going on the mission with him.

So do you want to go? Today? Jesus is still looking for apprentices in the 21st century. So why don't you go with him?

Do you think that following Jesus means following a list of rules? Do you think following Jesus means having the right beliefs? Perhaps you find it hard to follow someone that you can't see.

So how do you follow someone you can't see? You would need their words. And Jesus speaks to you through his words. The way you get to know God is through Jesus. The way you get to know Jesus is through his words as you go on the mission with him to help heal the world. He wants you to come. But he's not waiting.

## Day 6

# The mission starts with a Relationship.

### Jesus calls Peter and Andrew

*Jesus called out to them, "Come, follow me, and I will show you how to fish for people!" And they left their nets at once and followed him." Matthew 4:19-20 (NLT)*

Follow me. With two words Jesus invites you not only to change the world but to get to know him. Jesus offers unlikely apprentices like you and fishermen like Peter and Andrew a relationship – a friendship. But it's even more than that, you don't choose Jesus, he chooses you.

Have you ever not been picked for something? Have you ever been passed over? Have you ever been rejected or ignored or simply failed at something? Peter and Andrew had. That's why Jesus' words: "follow me" meant so much to them.

In the days of Jesus, only the best and brightest students were chosen to become the future religious leaders. Oral tests were taken to demonstrate their knowledge of the Old Testament law and prophets. Those who passed the tests were approached by a rabbi who would say these words to them "Follow me." Those who didn't pass never heard those words.

Imagine if you were one of those who didn't get asked. How would you feel? You would probably either be mad at the religious leaders or mad at yourself – maybe a little of both – but either way you're tired of taking tests.

The apprentices that Jesus chose were not selected by the rabbis. They were not destined to be the future leaders of their people. They went out and got "regular" jobs. And yet, these are the ones who Jesus chose. Isn't it amazing? Jesus picked people who did not get picked! Jesus picked the people who had never heard the words: "Follow me." They were nobody's apprentice.

Does this make sense? Wouldn't you assume that if Jesus was the Messiah, He would pick the best and brightest students?

Can you see now why these words were so powerful? Can you see why they left everything? Can you see why you would, too? Think what it meant to them then and what it means to you today.

*Follow me.* Jesus accepts you for who you are. Until now, when you thought about God, you felt rejection – that you did not measure up to the standards of the religious leaders. You felt rejected by God. You were rejected by others, who are in some ways still rejecting you. In two words, Jesus says – I know who you are and I accept you.

*Follow me.* Jesus thinks you have something to offer the world. Jesus chooses you. Yes, you – the unlikely apprentice. He thinks that you were uniquely designed to have an important role in his mission to change the world. Jesus sees something in you that you may not even see in yourself.

*Follow me*. Jesus wants a relationship with you. For most of your life, you've thought the religious leaders were the most spiritual, but you certainly didn't want to be around them. And they certainly did not want to be around you.

Then you meet someone who is even more spiritual than anyone that you have ever met and to your surprise you actually like him. You want to be around him. And he wants to be around you. You become friends.

*Follow me.* Jesus promises to make you something that you cannot make yourself. That on this mission to change the world, you will become the person you've always wanted to be. Follow me and I would make you what you cannot make yourself.

For most of your life, religious leaders have told you, "Follow this . . . follow that . . . do this . . . don't do that." Jesus says, "Follow me," not, "Follow this." For the first time, you think that God cares more about you than religious rules.

You've always believed that God loves you but you've been led to believe that keeping religious rules was the only way to love him back.

And now...you're starting to figure out that Jesus wants even more. He wants you. He doesn't just love you; He likes you. He knows everything (good and bad) that you've done, and he likes you.

The mission starts with a relationship.

### The Big Idea:
Jesus likes you.

### Question:
What does a relationship with Jesus look like today?

### Think about Jesus' words
*Jesus called out to them, "Come, follow me, and I will show you how to fish for people!"*
*Matthew 4:19 (NLT)*

## Day 7
# Jesus invites you into His Life

### Jesus is Life

*...the Word gave life to everything that was created, and his life brought life to everyone. John 1:4 (NLT)*

### Jesus offers life to dead people

*Anyone here who believes what I am saying right now and aligns himself with the Father...has at this very moment the real, lasting life...this person has taken a giant step from the world of the dead to the world of the living.*
*John 5:24 (Message)*

Jesus invites you into his life. Yet isn't it more likely for you to hear someone say that they invited Jesus into their life. Maybe you've even been asked if you want Jesus to come into your heart and wondered what that looks like?

Do you open a tiny, miniature door to your heart and a little miniature Jesus walks in? If you are like me, that is the picture you have.

As a child, I remember being asked if I wanted Jesus to come live in my heart so that I could go to heaven. And though I was only five, I knew enough at that point that I certainly did not want to go to hell and that heaven was the preferred destination.

I said, "Yes." In my mind, I opened the miniature door to my heart and this miniature Jesus came into my life (see Revelation 3:20). I had invited Jesus into my life. I could prove it. Miniature Jesus lived inside of me.

From that day forward, Miniature Jesus went everywhere I went. There were times that I sensed that he disapproved of where I was going or what I was doing and this led to some conflict. Miniature Jesus and I argued about my decision making. And in the end, sometimes I listened and sometimes I didn't. Even though I didn't always listen, I was always glad he was there – especially when tempted.

In temptation, I would pray to Miniature Jesus to help me out – to give me the power to overcome these urges and desires. In most cases, Miniature Jesus was not quite powerful enough to keep me from doing what I wanted to do but wished I didn't want to (see Romans 7). Sometimes I felt guilty doing things that I knew did not please him. Other times I thought that Miniature Jesus would just understand.

As I grew older, I asked Miniature Jesus for direction. "What is your will for my life," I asked him. Miniature Jesus rarely told me straight out. So, I usually went the way of the first open door and thanked him for the sign.

There were times that I got the opportunity to share Miniature Jesus with my friends. I was always a little embarrassed talking about him, because he was so small. But in the end, I thought they should invite Miniature Jesus into their life, too. It was better than going to hell.

Life with Miniature Jesus was fine - the only problem was that he didn't seem real. He also didn't seem powerful enough to change the world – he couldn't even change me. And he was also very different from the Jesus the apprentices followed and the Jesus you want to follow.

What does the real Jesus look like? What does it mean to come into his life?

**Come into my life.** Jesus is not trying to follow you. Jesus didn't go up to Peter, James, and John and say, "Hey, guys where are you going? Can I come, too?" And in the same way, Jesus isn't wondering where you're going and if you have room for him in your life."

The real Jesus says, *"Anyone who intends to come with me has to let me lead. You're not in the driver's seat; I am." (Matthew 16:24 Message)*

Following Jesus means you give him the steering wheel of your life. Miniature Jesus doesn't lead – you lead him. The real Jesus leads. He leads and you follow. He teaches and you obey.

**Come into my life.** Jesus lives out his mission through the lives of his apprentices. *"Christ lives in me. The life you see me living is not 'mine,' but it is lived by faith in the Son of God, who loved me and gave himself for me." (Galatians 2:20 Message)*

It's not that Jesus doesn't want to live in your heart. Rather, it is that Jesus gets into your heart when you come into his life and go on the mission with him.

The dominant teaching throughout the New Testament is that Jesus apprentices are "in Christ (Greek: en Christos)." *(If anyone is <u>in Christ</u>, they are a new creation." 2 Corinthians 5:17)* These two words – in Christ – describe the new life the followers of Jesus live.

Miniature Jesus cannot get you on the mission and cannot make you a new person. The real Jesus does.

**Come into my life**. Jesus' life lasts forever. Jesus offered more than a better existence on earth. He did not offer human life (Greek: bios – to exist). He offered eternal life (Greek: zoe – to be alive).

He says, *"I am, right now, Resurrection and Life. The one who believes in me does not ultimately die at all. Do you believe this?" (John 11:25 Message)*

When you come into Jesus' Life, he gives you life that never ends. When your heart stops pumping here, and it is the end of your human life – it is not the end of Jesus' life and it is not the end of your spiritual life.

He says to his apprentices, *"I'm on my way to get your room ready, and I'll come back and get you so that you can live where I live." (John 14:3 Message)*

Jesus apprentices have life forever and live together with him in a new heaven and new earth. Miniature Jesus cannot give you life forever. The real Jesus does.

*That is why whoever accepts and trusts the Son gets in on everything, life complete and forever. (John 3:36 Message)*

**Come into my life**. Jesus' life forever (zoe) starts today. He promises, *"Real, lasting life…a giant step from the world of the dead to the world of the living."* (John 5:24 Message)

The moment that you come into Jesus' life you start really living. You come alive. Only the real Jesus – not Miniature Jesus – can make you come alive.

*"Whoever believes in me has real life, eternal life." (John 6:47 Message)*

***Come into my life.*** Jesus' life is much bigger than yours. On the mission, you get to see the world Jesus sees. You get to see just how big the huge problems of the world are and how passionate Jesus is to solve them. You see God at work in the world.

This is the adventure you get to go on when you come into Jesus' life and go on the mission with him.

So...do you want the real Jesus?

## The Big Idea:

Jesus invites you into his life.

## Question:

How does Jesus' life make your life different?

## Think about Jesus' words

*"Anyone here who believes what I am saying right now and aligns himself with the Father...has at this very moment the real, lasting life." John 5:24 (Message)*

## Day 8
# Jesus isn't trying to make you religious

### Jesus responds to criticism from religious leaders

*Jesus, overhearing, shot back, "Who needs a doctor: the healthy or the sick? Go figure out what this Scripture means: 'I'm after mercy not religion.' I'm here to invite outsiders, not coddle insiders." Matthew 9:12-13 (Message)*

### Jesus invites Peter and Andrew to change

*Jesus said to them, "Come with me. I'll make a new kind of fisherman out of you. I'll show you how to catch men and women instead of perch and bass."*
*Matthew 4:19-20 (Message)*

Jesus' offer to his apprentices is simply this: "Come with me...I will make a new kind of fisherman out of you."

Jesus isn't trying to make you more religious. Jesus isn't trying to make you happy with everything this world has to offer. Jesus wants to make you more like him – someone who loves people.

I've always wondered what Jesus' words 'catch men and women' meant to Peter and Andrew because they mean nothing to me. What about you? Are you interested in God turning you into a people-catcher? How would this offer cause reasonable people like Peter, Andrew, James, and

John to leave their jobs as commercial fisherman to follow Jesus? What if you were one of these fishermen? Would you go? What does it mean to become a fisher of men?

**Jesus makes you a fisher of men**. Jesus changes what you care about. Speaking your language, Jesus told you fishermen that he would re-frame what is important to you. As a fisherman, he knew that your whole life had become about the number of fish you could catch. Your nets would determine your net worth which would determine your self-worth.

The major change for you is that your life is no longer about "stuff." Your life is going to be about people. Jesus will make you into a person who cares more about people you meet than fish you catch.

**Jesus makes you a fisher of men**. Jesus changes who your role-models are. Instead of wanting to become like the person with the largest fishing boat, the best fisherman, or the person with the biggest catch--you want to become like Jesus – someone who attracts people to God.

Think about it. You were never even tempted to become like the religious leaders, but now you have left everything to follow Jesus. Why? Jesus attracts you to God. He makes you hungry for God's Kingdom on earth. He makes you into an authentic spiritual leader. Wow. This is so different. You always considered yourself a business person or an athlete – but a spiritual leader? No way. But Jesus inspires you to want to become someone who attracts others to God and His Kingdom.

**Jesus makes you a fisher of men**. Jesus changes how you view the world. Instead of focusing on the outward things in life, Jesus turns your attention to people's hearts. You no longer think that the problems of the world are because there is no God. You used to say things like, "If there was a God then bad things wouldn't happen to good people," or "How could a loving God allow human suffering?"

Instead of asking, "Where's God," and blaming him for the mess in the world, you are on a mission with God to put the world right again.

You understand that the mess isn't God's doing and that just because a child's room is a mess, it doesn't necessarily mean that a parent doesn't exist. You don't blame the parent or assign the child a longer list of rules. You get involved in the transformation of this room starting with the change in the child's heart.

**Jesus makes you a fisher of men**. Jesus changes who you spend your time with. Religious leaders attract those who want religious rules. Rome attracts pleasure seekers who want more status and "stuff." Jesus attracts those who are hungry for what really matters in life. He attracts people who want unconditional love. And instead of telling you how bad you are, he tells you how loved you are. Being around Jesus makes you want to love people more.

Jesus did not attract religious people who weren't open to change and he didn't want to. In fact, he turned them off. Jesus spent time with people that the religious people did not associate with.

"What kind of example is this from your Teacher, acting cozy with crooks and riff-raff?" (Matthew 9:11 Message)

Jesus turned off the religious "insiders," and if you are on the mission with Jesus, you will probably turn them off, too.

Jesus, also, didn't attract self-centered pleasure seekers because you had to give up so much to follow him. He attracted spiritually hungry people who were "outsiders" to the religious leaders. He loved spending time with them. And being around Jesus makes you enjoy being with spiritually hungry people, too.

**Jesus makes you a fisher of men.** Jesus gives you a mission. You have something worth giving your life for. Instead of simply working to get to the weekend, you live every day in expectation of miracles – working with Jesus to change the world by changing people's hearts.

You aren't becoming more religious. You aren't becoming more like the pleasure seekers. You are becoming more like Jesus, and that's what he wants. Now you're on the mission together.

## The Big Idea:
Jesus wants to make you like him.

## Question:
How are you becoming more like Jesus?

## Think about Jesus' words
*"I'm after mercy not religion. I'm here to invite outsiders, not coddle insiders." Matthew 9:13 (Message)*

## Day 9
# Jesus teaches you to pray

### Jesus teaches his apprentices to pray

*Once Jesus was in a certain place praying. As he finished, one
of his disciples came to him and said, "Lord, teach us to pray."
Luke 11:1 (NLT)*

Jesus teaches you to pray like he does. When Jesus came
into our world there were plenty of people who prayed just
like there are plenty of people who pray today. Do you pray?

You've heard people pray, you might have even prayed with
them, and you probably pray by yourself. Whether it's
before a meal, at the end of the day, when someone is sick,
you're in trouble, or at a wedding or funeral, prayer is
nothing new to you. So why do you need Jesus to teach you
to pray?

Jesus has a personal connection to God that you don't have
– none of the apprentices do – at least to start. You know
how to say the words of prayer, but Jesus' prayers change
the world. After seeing people's lives healed right in front
of your eyes, you have to admit that you have never seen
anyone who can pray like Jesus prays. So, you ask Jesus to
teach you to pray. Would you like to learn how to pray from
Jesus himself?

*"Master, teach us to pray..." (Luke 11:1 Message)*

**Jesus teaches you to pray.** Prayer is simple and personal.

You pray to your Father in Heaven.

*"With a God like this loving you, you can pray very simply. Like this: Our Father in heaven, reveal who you are." (Matthew 6:9 Message)*

The Romans pray to their gods as a magical or mystical way of facing life. If you're Roman, you go to the temple (of your gods), bring an offering and hope that the gods are pleased.

It's similar to putting all your money on red (playing roulette) and hoping lady luck goes your way. You could call it "prayer poker" or "prayer power ball".

It's not hard for you to believe that people would try to use God to get money. And it's not hard for you to believe that people want to profit off of people wanting to pray.

In the Kingdom of Rome, the gods were not simple, they were complex. You never knew which side of the bed your gods would wake up on that day. Jesus does not want you to pray like the Romans do.

*"The world is full of so-called prayer warriors who are prayer-ignorant. They're full of formulas and programs and advice, peddling techniques for getting what you want from God. Don't fall for that nonsense." (Matthew 6:7 Message)*

The prayers of the religious leaders were public and professional. It was a show. Jesus called them *"… 'play actors'… – treating prayer meeting and street corner alike as a stage, acting compassionate as long as someone is watching, playing to the crowds." (Matthew 6:5 Message)*

The prayers in the Kingdom of Religion were not simple, they were long. They were not relational; they tried to impress everyone with how spiritual they were. Their prayers were fancy.

Jesus blows you away when he says to call God, "Dad" (Aramaic, Abba). Prayer becomes personal because you're actually praying to someone who knows you. Do you pray to God like he knows you? You can. God doesn't just know you; he cares deeply about you. So, when you pray, keep it simple and speak from the heart.

**Jesus teaches you to pray.** Prayer is about what God wants, not what you want.

*"May your Kingdom come soon. May your will be done on earth, as it is in heaven." (Matthew 6:10 NLT)*

Jesus teaches you that prayer is not so you can get God on your side, but so he can get you on his. Prayer changes the world because God changes your heart. In prayer, God prepares you for the mission by getting you on the same page with him. Are you getting it? Jesus changes the world by changing people's heart. With prayer, it starts with you.

**Jesus teaches you to pray.** Prayer is a way of putting your faith in God to meet your everyday needs.

*"Give us today the food we need…" (Matthew 6:11 NLT)*

Instead of hoping for the gods to accept your offering and answer your prayers or trying to say all the right words so that God will hear you, Jesus teaches you to go directly to God for your needs. Are you asking with a simple heart?

You may be one of those people who think that you can't pray well enough so you need to go to a professional to say it for you. But Jesus doesn't think so. You don't have to be a prayer expert. In fact, the professional may get in the way. God wants to hear your voice and your heart, not something filtered through a professional. I mean, would you want to have your attorney send a love letter for you? You get the point. Jesus knows you can pray to God directly by yourself.

*"Here's what I want you to do: Find a quiet, secluded place so you won't be tempted to role-play before God. Just be there as simply and honestly as you can manage. The focus will shift from you to God, and you will begin to sense his grace." (Matthew 6:6 Message)*

**Jesus teaches you to pray.** Prayer is about getting your heart right.

*"And forgive us our sins, as we have forgiven those who sin against us." (Matthew 6:12 NLT)*

Jesus teaches you that prayer is a way for God to work on your heart so that your relationships with the people around you are pleasing to him. Is there a tense relationship in your life? Have you prayed about it? Maybe you prayed for God to change them, but what he wants to do is change you. This is why Jesus knows that prayer changes the world, because God changes your heart in prayer.

**Jesus teaches you to pray.** Prayer is protection and keeping your heart sensitive to danger.

*"And don't let us yield to temptation but rescue us from the evil one." (Matthew 6:13 NLT)*

You are developing through prayer a personal connection with God that keeps you spiritually alive so you don't fall into temptation. You will also become far more aware of spiritual forces in the world.

By staying connected to God in prayer, you learn how to make wise choices to avoid temptation as well as overcoming it.

*"Keep watch and pray, so that you will not give in to temptation. For the spirit is willing, but the body is weak!" (Matthew 26:41 NLT)*

**Jesus teaches you to pray.** Prayer is about how big God is and how his Kingdom comes into this world through our hearts.

*"Yours is the Kingdom, and the Power, and the Glory, forever"*

Jesus teaches you to pray in a way that changes the way you look at the world. And both you and the world will never be the same.

## The Big Idea:
Jesus teaches you to pray.

## Question:
How can prayer become part of your everyday life?

## Think about Jesus' words
*"With a God like this loving you, you can pray very simply. Like this: Our Father in heaven, reveal who you are."*
*Matthew 6:7-8 (Message)*

## Day 10
# The change starts inside of You

### Jesus and Nicodemus

*I tell you the truth, unless you are born again, you cannot see the Kingdom of God. John 3:3 (NLT)*

### Jesus explains how His Kingdom arrives.

*The Kingdom of God doesn't come by counting the days on the calendar. Nor when someone says, 'Look here!' or, 'There it is!' And why? Because God's kingdom is already among you.*
*Luke 17:20 (Message)*

The change starts inside of you. It's easy to spot the problems of the world – they are huge! It's not hard to spot the problems in the people around you – they are obvious. But what about you? Do you have any blind spots?

It's definitely easier to see others blind spots than our own! Jesus called others blind spots "specks" or "sawdust"— while humorously pointing out our own blind spots when he said: *"And why worry about a speck in your friend's eye when you have a log in your own?" (Matthew 7: 3 NLT)*

However, Jesus' plan to change the world by changing people's hearts starts inside of you. This is especially hard to swallow if you see yourself as one of the people who actually doesn't need changing.

Late one night, a religious leader named Nicodemus (the

original Nick at Nite), came to Jesus. We don't really know whether it was because he didn't want to be seen with Jesus or simply that he wanted an opportunity to speak with Jesus uninterrupted. One thing we do know: Nicodemus was curious.

Even the religious leaders like Nicodemus can see that there is something unique about Jesus. You could debate with him about his teachings, perhaps shame him for the people he hung around with, but you couldn't argue with the miracles he performed.

Nicodemus starts off by saying, *"Rabbi, we all know you're a teacher straight from God. No one could do all the God-pointing, God-revealing acts you do if God weren't in on it." (John 3:2 Message)*

Jesus responds, "You're absolutely right...I'm pointing – to God's kingdom." *(John 3:3 Message)*

This had to be a bit exhilarating for Nicodemus. Like others, he was hoping the Messiah ("Christ" in the Greek) would come to free them from the Roman Empire and usher in God's Kingdom. (And having a Messiah with miraculous powers could really come in handy.)

Then Jesus tells this religious leader that unless something changes in Nicodemus, he won't actually see God's Kingdom. Ever!

*Unless a person is born from above, it's not possible to see...God's Kingdom. (John 3:3 Message)*

Nicodemus is shocked...not see the Kingdom...I don't want to miss that! In his human head, Nicodemus can't see that Jesus is talking about a Kingdom that is larger than just Israel – it's for everyone. And the way it comes to this world is not by conquering the Romans or forcing the Kingdom on others (like the Crusades). God's Kingdom comes first in your heart. This is the only way to really change the world.

You have to be…what? Born from above? *"How can you be born when you're already grown up? You can't re-enter your mother's womb and be born again." (John 3:4 Message)*

You can imagine…Nicodemus the religious leader, the one who passed the tests, the scholar, trying to figure this one out. "Born from above" …what does that mean?

**You have to be born from above**. Until you become a new person you really won't get the mission that Jesus is on – and God is not going to make sense to you. You'll either be wondering: "Where is God" or "Why are people so bad." You won't see God's Kingdom, let alone live in it.

*"You're not listening. Let me say it again. Unless a person submits to this original creation…a baptism into a new life – it's not possible to enter God's Kingdom." (John 3:5 Message)*

**You have to be born from above**. Living in God's Kingdom means that Jesus becomes your leader – the director of your life.

Then Jesus reveals the motive of His mission to Nicodemus: *"This is how much God loved the world: He gave his Son, his one and only Son. And this is why: so that no one need be destroyed; by believing in him, anyone can have a whole and lasting life."* (John 3:16 Message)"

The one and only reason that Jesus is on this mission is love. That's it. Jesus wants to change the world because God loves people. God loves you.

Jesus put it this way to Nicodemus, *"God didn't go to all the trouble of sending his Son merely to point an accusing finger, telling the*

*world how bad it was. He came to help, to put the world right again."*
*(John 3:17 Message)*

**You have to be born from above**. Living in God's Kingdom means Jesus becomes your healer – the forgiver of your life. Jesus takes Nicodemus back to a moment of healing in their national history when Moses lifted up a serpent for all to look on and be healed.

In the same way, Jesus says that he must be lifted up and…
*"Everyone who looks up to him, trusting and expectant, will gain a real life, eternal life." (John 3:15 Message)*

**You have to be born from above**. Living in God's Kingdom means Jesus becomes your life – the power to live a life that please God. Jesus tells Nicodemus at night, come out of the darkness and into the light.

*"God-light streamed into the world, but men and women everywhere ran for the darkness…everyone who makes a practice of doing evil, addicted to denial and illusion, hates God-light and won't come near it…but anyone working and living in truth and reality welcomes God-light so the work can be seen for the God-work it is." (John 3:19-21 Message)*

So…what ever happened to Nicodemus? Something happened . . . because after watching Jesus die on the cross, Nicodemus is one of two people who takes Jesus off the cross to be placed in a tomb.

When all of Jesus' apprentices had run away, Nicodemus stepped forward…and this time it wasn't at night…it was in the daylight.

*Nicodemus, who had first come to Jesus at night, came now in broad daylight… (John 19:39 Message)*

Nicodemus was born from above and he would never be the same. He was a follower of Jesus.

What about you? Has the change started in your heart?

Jesus isn't trying to get you to agree with him on a list of beliefs. He isn't trying to convert you to a religion – even the religion of Christianity (if there is such a thing). Jesus isn't trying to get you to say a certain prayer so that you can go to heaven. Jesus isn't trying to make your life better.

Jesus invites you to follow – to go on the mission with him to change the world by changing people's hearts. You either go or you don't. And the only way to go is for the change to start inside of you. To go on the mission, you have to get your own heart on the mission first.

The question isn't whether you're religious or not. The question is not whether you consider yourself a Christian or not. The question is: are you on the mission with Jesus. That's it.

The Pharisees knew the belief statement – they could quote it – they could quote the entire Law. But they weren't on the mission. Their hearts were not on the mission. They loved their laws more than they loved people…. more than they loved God. And they were never going to see God's Kingdom.

The Romans were not on the mission. They were on their own mission. Their lives were busy stuffing themselves with the best the world could offer trying to be happy. And their Kingdom crumbled…

Do you find yourself in the Kingdom of Rome or the Kingdom of Religion? Do you want out? Have you had enough of pleasure seeking and rule keeping? What if you went on the mission with Jesus?

There are no magic words and there is no formula. Jesus is on a mission. Do you want to go with him? It's yes or no.

If you want to go too, I encourage you to tell him in your own words right now. Say yes.

"Yes Jesus, I want to go on the mission with you. Start in my heart. Change me from the inside out. Teach me how to love. Teach how to bring your Kingdom to this world. I come into your life. I choose to follow you."

*"Say the welcoming word to God, - Jesus is my Master – embracing, body and soul, God's work of doing in us what He did in raising Jesus from the dead. That's it." (Romans 10:9 Message)*

## The Big Idea:
The change starts inside of your heart.

## Question:
What are some of the changes that going on the mission with Jesus will mean in your life?

## Think about Jesus' words
*"I tell you the truth, unless you are born again, you cannot see the Kingdom of God." John 3:3 (NLT)*

**Week Three**
# Practice #2:
# Jesus shows us
# the Good Life

### Jesus on trial before Pilate
*My Kingdom is not an earthly kingdom.*
*John 18:36 (NLT)*

## Introduction
## Week Three

What does a perfect world look like? Can you imagine it? God can-and Jesus came to show us what it looks like and how to live in it. It's called the good life.

What do you think is the good life?

Maybe you think the good life is having it all. So, you've been trying to create your own version of heaven on earth. Maybe you think that this world is literally going to hell. You're trying to endure this life so you can live the good life in heaven. Jesus thinks you are still in this world so you can learn how to live the good life here.

Jesus came to show you how to live out the good life on earth, so that you actually know how to live the good life in the new heavens and new earth forever. Impossible? It is on your own. But when Jesus invites you into his life, he gives you his Spirit. The Holy Spirit empowers you and teaches you how to live the good life.

Jesus calls the good life – the Kingdom of God or the Kingdom of Heaven. It's totally different than the Kingdom of Rome and the Kingdom of Religion. It starts in our hearts, and it's so different that when you live the good life everybody around you knows it. It's so different that you actually have to repent—turn around and move in a new direction-- to live in it. You end up standing out like a light in darkness. In fact, you bring glory to God making others hungry for it too.

So, what does the good life look like? Follow Jesus and find out.

## Day 11
# The Good Life
# is totally Different

### The Theme of Jesus' Campaign
*Change your life. God's Kingdom is here.*
*Matthew 4:17 (Message)*

The good life changes the world because it changes you. The good life is what Jesus lived out with his apprentices. He calls it the Kingdom of God. Jesus came to earth to show you how to live in his Kingdom. The theme for Jesus' campaign to change the world was simply: *"Change your life. God's Kingdom is here."*

Can you imagine being one of those people in Jesus' hometown, Nazareth when Jesus reads from one of the ancient sacred scrolls (Isaiah 61) about the coming Messiah and the Kingdom of God and then he sits down and says, *"The Scripture you've just heard has been fulfilled this very day! (Luke 4:21 NLT)*

This is Jesus saying, "Hello, everyone – I'm the Messiah! I'm ready to change the world now – let's roll."

Sounds great and all, Jesus, but…um…like, we know who your parents are…and we watched you grow up. So how about you sit down, and next time pick a different part of the scriptures to read in the synagogue.

These people were upset. And that's an understatement. They were ready to kill him.

*"They threw him out, banishing him from the village, then took him to a mountain cliff at the edge of the village to throw him to his doom." (Luke 4:29 Message)*

So how does Jesus respond to the people he grew up with wanting to kill him? He walks right through this angry mob and right into the mission. And everywhere Jesus goes – this is his message – *"Change your life now, God's Kingdom is here."*

It also becomes your message as Jesus' apprentice. When it comes time for Jesus to send you and the other apprentices out, he tells you to stick to the theme of his campaign.

*"He commissioned them to preach the news of God's Kingdom and heal the sick." (Luke 9:2 Message)*

When Jesus sends you out in a larger team of apprentices, the seventy-two, guess what he tells you to say?

*"Heal anyone who is sick, and tell them, "God's Kingdom is right at your doorstep!" (Luke 10:9 Message)*

Bringing the Kingdom of God to this world is the mission. The good life – the Kingdom of God – changes our world. And it's at your doorstep.

This is exciting news for you because you have been waiting for this day to arrive. However, it is hard for you to not be a bit cynical.

The Kingdom of God is here? Where? Everywhere you look all you can see is the Kingdom of Rome. How is Jesus going to bring God's Kingdom? It's not like the Roman Empire is going to be "okay" with that. As if Caesar is going to say, "Yeah, sure Jesus – why don't you and your people take that little area over there in Palestine. You can have your

Kingdom there."

But what you don't realize is that Jesus has a different idea of what his Kingdom is all about. What is the Kingdom of God? And how do you get to live in it?

**You have to change your life now.** The Kingdom of God is not about you.

The Kingdom of Rome offers you its version of the good life – focusing on what you want. The problem with this version of the good life is…it's far from good. Many times, it brings out some really bad things in you like lust, greed, and pride. This selfish living destroys you, your relationships, and the world you live in.

The Kingdom of Religion offered you its version of the good life – also known as the "how to be good" manual. You try your best to live by this manual, but it doesn't make you good. It may make your sins less obvious – at least to you – but in the end your heart is not changed. Not only is this version of the good life not attractive to you, it isn't attractive to others. Nobody wants it. And nobody brings glory to God that way.

Neither of these kingdoms have the power to change the world because they can't change you. Both Kingdoms are still about you. The focus in both is you. How you can be happy. How you can be a better person.

God's Kingdom and Your Kingdom cannot exist together, because the good life teaches you the very opposite: that it's not about you.

*Then Jesus said to his disciples, "if any of you wants to be my follower, you must give up your own way, take up your cross, and follow me."*
*(Matthew 16:24 NLT)*

**You have to change your life now.** You have to admit to yourself that the Kingdom of Rome will never satisfy you. Deep down you know it's true, but you have to admit it. Jesus tells you the truth about the Kingdom of Rome.

*"And what do you benefit if you gain the whole world but lose your own soul? Is anything worth more than your soul?" (Matthew 16:26 NLT)*

Once you give up on the idea that if you just got that next vacation, that next job, that next relationship, or that next big break, you are ready to experience what really satisfies you. You are ready for the good life--a life focused on God and his passion to love the people of the world.

**You have to change your life now.** The good life is about learning to love. Jesus teaches you this by loving you and being your friend.

*"There is no greater love than to lay down one's life for one's friends." (John 15:13 NLT)*

Once you are free from the thought that life is about you, you are ready to care about people and the huge problems of the world. Think about all the energy you use up every day on yourself. Now you have all of that energy freed up to focus on others. As soon as you begin to focus on other people, your heart begins to care about them – and you start to learn how to love.

**You have to change your life now.** The Kingdom of God is a totally different way to live, love, and think. This total change is called repentance, a 180-degree-turn, an about-face of your heart. And, it's awesome.

## The Big Idea:
The good life is totally different.

## Question:
How can you make your life more about God and others?

## Think about Jesus' words
*"Change your life. God's Kingdom is here."*
*Matthew 3:2 (Message)*

## Day 12
# The Good Life is perfect

### Jesus raises the bar

*But I warn you – unless your righteousness is better than the righteousness of the teachers of religious law and the Pharisees, you will never enter the Kingdom of Heaven!*
*Matthew 5:20 (NLT)*

### Jesus' standard

*But you are to be perfect, even as your Father in heaven is perfect. Matthew 5:48 (NLT)*

The good life is perfect. Can you imagine what a perfect life looks like? This may be hard for you to imagine. It was hard for people in Jesus' day, so the religious leaders tried to list out the rules for a perfect life.

You see, the religious leaders focused completely on keeping the law – their religious rules – and making sure that everyone else was keeping them, too. They added more rules to help people better keep the laws they already had. Most of their writings dealt with dietary law, circumcision, and Sabbath-keeping.

The religious leaders taught that keeping these laws was the pathway to a perfect life. They also taught that if everyone could perfectly keep these laws, the Messiah would come and change the world.

For most of the people, these extra rules were impossibly complex and hard to remember let alone keep. It was difficult living in a community where your every move was under a microscope with people waiting to catch you in a mistake.

Can you imagine living in a world where people actually want to catch you doing things wrong so they can penalize you? Would it make you want to try harder or give up? Many people in Jesus' day simply gave up on the idea that you could actually please God. The bar was simply too high.

Then Jesus comes into the world, sits everyone down for his famous message (the Sermon on the Mount) and basically says that the problem with the bar isn't that it's too high, but too low.

What? Too low? Yes, too low.

*"But I warn you — unless your righteousness is better than the righteousness of the teachers of religious law and the Pharisees, you will never enter the Kingdom of Heaven!" (Matthew 5:20 NLT)*

Stop. Are you saying, Jesus, that if we don't do even better than the religious leaders that we won't enter the Kingdom of God? There's no chance then. And what about them? They've got to do better, too? How?

**The good life is perfect.** Jesus teaches you that everyone needs God's grace — even the religious leaders. The standards in the Kingdom of God are this: *"But you are to be perfect, even as your Father in heaven is perfect." Matthew 5:48 NLT)*

Wow…perfect…like your Heavenly Father is? Jesus makes it sound like perfectly keeping the laws isn't enough. The good life is becoming perfect like your Heavenly Father. And if that's true, nobody has arrived yet.

**The good life is perfect.** Jesus' standards are higher. They are higher because only God can perfectly live them for you and your heart has to change to embrace what he does for you.

Look at it this way: The problem is not violence but hate. The standard is higher. Do not murder – that is not a standard – that is the minimum for humane living. The problem is in your heart.

*"You're familiar with the commands of the ancients, 'Do not murder.' I'm telling you that anyone who is so much as angry with a brother or sister is guilty of murder." (Matthew 5:21-22 Message)*

Murder? You would never kill anyone – what is Jesus talking about? Jesus teaches you what you already know in your heart – words kill.

*"Thoughtlessly, yell 'Stupid!' at a sister and you are on the brink of hellfire." (Matthew 5:22 Message)*

Here's another one: The problem is not adultery but lust. The standard is higher. Jesus says the standard is not simply "Don't have sex with someone you are not married to." No, that is not a standard – that is a minimum for humane living. The problem is in your heart.

*"You have heard the commandment that says, 'You must not commit adultery.' But I say, anyone who even looks at a woman with lust has already committed adultery with her in his heart." (Matthew 5:27-28 NLT)*

Never lust? Is there anyone who can say – "actually I guess I'm perfect on that one?" At this point, you start thinking – wow, all of us need God's grace. And the religious leaders start wondering the same thing about themselves.

Jesus takes the two commandments that most religious

leaders think they have never broken and shows them how they break the heart of the law all the time.

But Jesus doesn't stop there: The problem is not divorce but marriage. In Jesus' day, adultery was frowned on by the Jewish culture. So, how do you get around it if you want to drop your wife and run off with another woman? According to their Law, you simply needed to get a certificate of divorce which many of the religious leaders did. This way they could be righteous and speak out against other people's unrighteousness.

Jesus reminds you: The standard is not "keep it legal" – that is the minimum for humane living – the standard is higher.

*"Remember the Scripture that says, 'whoever divorces his wife, let him do it legally, giving her divorce papers and her legal right?' Too many of you are using that as a cover for selfishness and whim, pretending to be righteous just because you are legal. (Matthew 5:31 Message)*

What is the standard for marriage? Jesus models it for you by dying for the church (also known as the Bride of Christ). The standard is the man who will die for his wife and the woman who will honor her husband.

**The good life is perfect.** The problem is not your mouth but your action. The standard is not "don't break your promises" – that is the minimum for humane living – the standard is higher – it's to be a person who doesn't have to make them.

*"And don't say anything you don't mean...in making your speech sound more religious, it becomes less true. Just say, 'yes' and 'no'." (Matthew 5:33, 37 Message)*

**The good life is perfect.** The standard is not how other people treat you; it's how you treat other people. The standard is not pay-backs, it's pay it forward (grace).

*"...If someone slaps you on the right cheek, offer the other cheek also...if a soldier demands that you carry his gear for a mile, carry it two miles." (Matthew 5:39-41 NLT)*

**The good life is perfect.** The problem is not that you don't love your friends – you don't love your enemies. That's the standard – how do you treat your enemies.

*"I'm telling you to love your enemies. Let them bring out the best in you, not the worst. When someone gives you a hard time, respond with the energies of prayer..." (Matthew 5:44 Message)*

After Jesus says all of this, you can see clearly how good the good life is...well, perfect...so perfect that nobody can live it out – nobody...except Jesus. And when you come into Jesus' life, you get Jesus' heart. Imagine millions – no billions – of people on the mission to change the world – all with Jesus' heart.

## The Big Idea:
The good life is perfect.

## Question:
What are some things in your heart that you want
Jesus to deal with?

## Think about Jesus' words
*"Grow up. You're kingdom subjects. Now live like it. Live out
your God-created identity. Live generously and graciously
towards others, the way God lives towards you."*
*Matthew 5:48 (Message)*

## Day 13
# The Standard in the Good Life is Love

### The Greatest Commandment

*And you must love the Lord your God with all your heart, all your soul, all your mind, and all your strength. The second is equally important: Love your neighbor as yourself. No other commandment is greater than these. Mark 12:30-31 (NLT)*

The standard in the good life is love. If there is any question what to do in a given situation, in the Kingdom of God the highest standard is love. If you get love right you will get all the commands right, too.

When asked what the greatest commandment was, Jesus didn't list off any of the Ten Commandments, he said two – loving God and loving people. If you do these two, you will not break any of the Ten.

In the Kingdom of God, the greatest commandment is: *"And you must love the Lord your God with all your heart, all your soul, all your mind, and all your strength. The second is equally important: Love your neighbor as yourself. No other commandment is greater than these." Mark 12:30-31 (NLT)*

The first part of this greatest commandment does not surprise you. It is a quote from one of your forefathers, Moses, called the Shema. You and your people would regularly quote this as part of your daily routine.

But then Jesus connects this with "love your neighbor". Somehow in Jesus' mind, these two are connected. In the Kingdom of God, you can't love God and not love your neighbor. It's impossible. And it's also impossible to live the good life without both of them.

So of course, an expert in the law asked Jesus, "Who is my neighbor?" If you were an expert in the law, you wanted to know this. The right interpretation of the rules would help you catch infractions.

Jesus responds with a story that is known as the story of the Good Samaritan. In the story, you are on a trip when you get beaten, robbed, and left for dead.

*They stripped him of his clothes, beat him up, and left him half dead beside the road. (Luke 10:30 NLT)*

Jesus continues the story with a priest and then another religious leader heading down the same road. These are two people who are very careful about keeping all the rules.

At the sight of the religious leaders, you are relieved thinking – finally, someone who can help. They see you in need but they "pass on the other side."

Why? Jesus doesn't say. Maybe they are concerned for their safety. Maybe they are concerned that you are dead and by touching you, they would become unclean.

As Jesus continues the story, the religious leaders are liking it less.

The third person on the road that you see is a Samaritan. Historically, there is racial tension between the Samaritans and your people. You hate them. Why?

The Samaritans were half-breeds in your mind. 1,000 years ago, your people lived in a divided Kingdom – the North and South. The capital of the Northern Kingdom was Samaria. When the Northern Kingdom was toppled with the fall of Samaria in 722 BC, many of those who lived there married into the surrounding nations.

Here comes the twist. A person from the people group that you hate the most, saves your life.

*"Then a despised Samaritan came along, and when he saw the man, he felt compassion for him. Going over to him, the Samaritan soothed his wounds with olive oil and wine and bandaged them. Then he put the man on his own donkey and took him to an inn where he took care of him." (Luke 10:33-34 NLT)*

Before leaving, the Samaritan pays your hospital bills with the promise that if there are more bills, he will pay them, too.

Jesus looks right into the eyes of the expert in the law and asks, *"Now which of these three would you say was a neighbor to the man who was attacked by bandits?" (Luke 10:36 NLT)*

Who else could the religious leader say but the Samaritan? *The expert says, "The one who had mercy on him."*

*Then Jesus said, "Yes, now go and do the same." (Luke 10:37 NLT)*

The standard in the good life is love. You learn to love by putting yourself in someone else's shoes and doing what you would want them to do for you. The Golden Rule is Law in the Kingdom of God.

*"Do to others as you would like them to do to you." (Luke 6:31 NLT)*

Can you imagine a world in which people treat others as they would like to be treated? Jesus can. It's the good life. It's how everyone in the Kingdom of God lives.

The irony is that in the Kingdom of God, it's the person that you don't think loves God that really teaches you how to love. In the process you fall in love with them. And learn how to love God together.

## The Big Idea:
The standard in the good life is love.

## Question:
Who is your "neighbor"?

## Think about Jesus' words
*Do to others whatever you would like them to do to you.*
*Matthew 7:12 (NLT)*

## Day 14
# Jesus shows you how to Love

### Jesus at the Last Supper

*Let me give you a new command: Love one another. In the same way I loved you, you love one another. This is how everyone will recognize that you are my disciples – when they see the love you have for each other. John 13:34-35 (Message)*

Jesus shows you how to love. Jesus modeled it. He didn't just tell you – he showed you. He came to earth to show you the good life – the Kingdom of God – and teaches you how to live this out right here on earth.

When you go with Jesus on the mission you get front row seats to the good life, and you get to experience his love. Jesus' plan to change the world by changing people's hearts is to show you how to love by loving you. He shows you how to love by loving people you don't want to love.

So how does Jesus love? What makes Jesus' love any different than the love from the Kingdom of Rome or the love from the Kingdom of Religion?

***Jesus shows you how to love.*** Jesus notices you. In the Kingdom of Religion, you want to be noticed by everyone else. And you will do things just so people will notice you and be impressed. You don't want to give attention; you want the attention. Jesus pointed out how the religious leaders wanted everyone to notice them.

*"Be especially careful when you are trying to be good so that you don't make a performance out of it. It might be good theater, but the God who made you won't be applauding." (Matthew 6:1 Message)*

In the Kingdom of Rome, you still want all the attention. Whether it's with what you wear or do, you want people to notice you. And in the Letter to the Romans, the Apostle Paul writes: *"Focusing on the self is the opposite to focusing on God. Anyone completely absorbed in self ignores God, ends up thinking more about self than God." (Romans 8:7 Message)*

Instead of bringing attention to himself, Jesus focused his attention on you. He noticed people, even when he wasn't noticed.

*"He was in the world, the world was there through him, and yet the world did not even notice." (John 1:10 Message)*

**Jesus shows you how to love.** Jesus embraces you right where you are. In the Kingdom of Religion, you were accepted when you obeyed the rules. In the Kingdom of Rome, you were accepted if you were one of them. How did Jesus accept you before you accepted him? By sitting down for a meal with you. Yes—a meal with Jesus.

When Jesus came into the world, acceptance was shown by who you would eat a meal with and who you would invite into your home. It was the very thing that the religious leaders and Romans would never do with people who were not one of them – people who they thought were below them.

On this mission with Jesus, you come to a tax collector that nobody likes. Jesus says to this tax collector, *"Today is my day to be a guest in your home." (Luke 19:5 Message)*

Jesus broke the rules of Religion for eating with the wrong

people.

*"This made the Pharisees and teachers of religious law complain that he was associating with such sinful people – even eating with them! (Luke 15:2 NLT)*

Why does Jesus eat with these people? Because he likes them. He accepts them. He loves them. And it isn't long until this type of acceptance cause people to open up and accept him.

***Jesus shows you how to love.*** Jesus stands up for you. In the Kingdom of Rome, people would stand up for you as long as you supported their government. In the Kingdom of Religion, people would stand up for you as long as you were in their religious party.

In the Kingdom of God, Jesus does things like standing up for people who everyone else is standing against. Jesus shows you how to love by standing up for you just like he stood up for the woman caught in the act of adultery.

Imagine you're that person caught, and you're standing trial before Jesus.

The religious leaders throw you down at Jesus' feet and say that you are guilty of an act that demands the death penalty. The religious law says that you must be killed (stoned to death).

*Jesus tells the religious leaders, "The sinless one among you; go first: throw the stone. (John 8:7 Message)*

One by one, everybody drops their stones and walks away, until it is just Jesus and you. Jesus says, *"Where are your accusers? Didn't even one of them condemn you? … Neither do I. Go and sin no more." (John 8:10-11 NLT)*

***Jesus shows you how to love.*** Jesus tells you the truth. In the Kingdom of Rome and the Kingdom of Religion, you would say one thing in front of people and another thing behind their back. Gossip, slander, and manipulation were part of the game. Jesus loved people enough to say what they needed to hear. He loved them enough that they actually heard it.

***Jesus shows you how to love.*** Jesus lays down His life for you. *"There is no greater love than to lay down one's life for one's friends." (John 15:13)*

In the good life, husbands lay down their lives for their wives by serving, and wives lay down their lives by submitting.

In the good life, parents lay down their lives by training their kids, and kids lay down their lives by honoring and obeying their parents.

In the good life, employees work as if their boss was God, and employers work as if they are going to be judged by him. Everyone lays down their life for each other.

*"And further, submit to one another out of reverence for Christ." (Ephesians 4:21 NLT)*

Jesus shows you how to love by loving you. And you show others how to love by loving them. This is how God's Kingdom comes to this world and Jesus changes the world by changing people's hearts.

Jesus shows you how to love because Jesus is love. And when we show others how to love by loving them, they get to see Jesus.

## The Big Idea:
Jesus shows us how to love.

## Question:
Who are some people that have shown you how to really love?

## Think about Jesus' words
*"There is no greater love than to lay down one's life for one's friends." John 15:13 (NLT)*

## Day 15

# Jesus' apprentices live out the Kingdom of God

### Jesus teaches His apprentices to pray

*With a God like this loving you, you can pray very simply.*
*Like this: Our Father in heaven, reveal who you are. Set the*
*world right; Do what's best – as above, so below.*
*Matthew 6:9-10 (Message)*

Jesus' apprentices live out the good life – the Kingdom of God. Jesus did not try to change the world alone. That wasn't his plan. Jesus called twelve non-religious followers on a mission with him and showed them a whole new world – the Kingdom of God.

The Kingdom of God has a totally different perspective on life than the Kingdom of Rome or the Kingdom of Religion.

Jesus sat his apprentices down before they went on their mission to unpack the message of the Kingdom of God (Sermon on the Mount). Jesus begins the message with the Beatitudes – the good life. His message describes how people in the Kingdom of God think and how different it is than Rome or the religious leaders.

***Jesus apprentices live out the good life***. Jesus teaches us that the poor in spirit are blessed.

*"You're blessed when you are at the end of your rope. With less of you, there is more of God and his rule." (Matthew 5:3 Message)*

The Romans thought you were blessed if you were rich and had everything you wanted. The Religious thought you were blessed if you were rich in rule-keeping and didn't really need much forgiveness.

In God's Kingdom, it is *"those who are forgiven much, who love much."*

***Jesus apprentices live out the good life.*** Jesus teaches us that those who mourn are blessed.

*"You're blessed when you feel you've lost what is most dear to you. Only then can you be embraced by the One most dear to you." (Matthew 5:4 Message)*

The Romans thought you were blessed if you had something amusing to laugh about. The Religious thought you were blessed if you had nothing to cry about. In God's Kingdom, pain in this life makes you long for life in the next. The good life is not being comfortable but comforting.

***Jesus apprentices live out the good life.*** Jesus teaches us that the meek are blessed.

*"You're blessed when you are content with just who you are - no more, no less. That's the moment that you find yourselves proud owners of everything that can't be bought." (Matthew 5:5 Message)*

The Romans thought the more you had the greater you were. The religious leaders thought the more you did the more honored you would be. In God's Kingdom, the goal is not to be great or to be honored – it is to make God's name great.

***Jesus apprentices live out the good life.*** Jesus teaches us those who hunger for righteousness are blessed.

*"You're blessed when you've worked up an appetite for God. He's food and drink in the best meal that you'll ever eat." (Matthew 5:6 Message)*

The Romans were hungry for sex, power, and money. The religious leaders were hungry for the applause and praise of people. In God's Kingdom, you begin to crave the things that this world cannot give you – you are hungry for a relationship with God that is real and alive.

***Jesus apprentices live out the good life***. Jesus teaches us that the merciful are blessed.

*"You're blessed when you care. At the moment of being 'care-full' you find yourself cared for." (Matthew 5:7 Message)*

The Romans thought that their greatest asset was their land and wealth. The religious leaders thought their greatest treasure was their temple. In God's Kingdom, the greatest treasure is the love and relationships you share with your friends...through Jesus.

***Jesus apprentices live out the good life.*** Jesus teaches us that the pure in heart are blessed.

*"You're blessed when you get your inside world – your mind and heart – put right. Then you will see God in the outside world." (Matthew 5:8 Message)*

The Romans worked at getting the outward stuff in their life right. The religious leaders worked to get the outward parts of the rules right. In God's Kingdom, you get your heart right first. Then you can see where God is at work around you.

***Jesus apprentices live out the good life***. Jesus teaches us that the peacemakers are blessed.

*"You're blessed when you can show people how to cooperate instead of compete or fight. That's when you discover who you really are, and your place in God's family." (Matthew 5:9 Message)*

The Romans thought that peace came through the Roman point of a sword. The religious leaders thought that peace came through the Messiah, the Warrior-King, who would lead them to victory in battle. In God's Kingdom, peace only comes through changing the hearts of people.

***Jesus apprentices live out the good life.*** Jesus teaches us that the persecuted are blessed.

*"You're blessed when your commitment to God provokes persecution. The persecution drives you even deeper into God's Kingdom." (Matthew 5:7 Message)*

The Romans thought they could stop the early followers of Jesus through persecution. The Religious thought they could stop the followers of Jesus through asking the Romans to persecute them. In God's Kingdom, the persecution moves the mission forward faster and stronger.

In a world in which the good life means having everything you want; Jesus teaches his apprentices to want the right things. The good life in the Kingdom of God is not only good on this earth, it's good for eternity. The Kingdom of God looks foolish to the Romans and weak to the Jews. But it is both the wisdom and power of God.

It is so different that it seems upside-down and backwards. Is it possible, though, that it's actually right-side up…and the future?

Jesus apprentices live out the Kingdom of God.

## The Big Idea:
Jesus apprentices live out God's Kingdom.

## Question:
What do you think the good life is?

## Think about Jesus' words
*"Our Father in heaven, hallowed be your name, your kingdom come, your will be done on earth as it is in heaven."*
*Matthew 6:8 (NKJV)*

## Week Four
# Practice #3:
# Jesus lives in the Culture

### God in a human body (The Incarnation)

*In the beginning the Word already existed. The Word was with God, and the Word was God. ...So the Word became human and made his home among us. He was full of unfailing love and faithfulness. And we have seen his glory, the glory of the Father's one and only Son. John 1:1, 14 (NLT)*

# Introduction
# Week Four

What would Jesus look like if he came today? Where would he live? What language would he speak? Who would be his friends? What do you think?

If the last time he came was any indication, Jesus would speak your language, live in your neighborhood, and you would be one of his friends.

Maybe you've always pictured Jesus as being too perfect to live in your world, that Jesus would be more comfortable around people who are more religious. He wasn't the last time he came.

Jesus was most comfortable living in the culture and loving the people in it. He refused to live in a religious bubble. Jesus likes the people in the culture, and he teaches you that you have to live in the culture to change it.

Jesus lives in the culture.

**Day 16**
# What's the difference between Jesus and religious leaders?

## Jesus tells his apprentices that he is different than religious leaders

*...I am the way, the truth, and the life. No one can come to the Father except through me.*
*John 14:6 (NLT)*

What's the difference between Jesus and religious leaders of his day? Was Jesus just better at it? What about other great religious leaders throughout history? How is he different than they are? Was Jesus a religious leader?

Jesus came into a world that already had religious leaders. There were four major Jewish religious groups and leaders in Jesus' day and all of them had a different way of dealing with the huge problems in their world.

The Pharisees thought that the problems in their world were due to people not obeying all the religious rules. They believed in a heaven and a hell and saw the world as an epic battle of good and evil with the culture as their enemy. If you were a Pharisees you thought that your people simply needed to get back to the religion of your forefathers, forgetting your forefathers weren't exactly perfect.

The Sadducees mixed into the culture and the Roman way of life. They didn't go as far as believing in an afterlife and thought that life would be best lived working with the Romans. If you were a Sadducee, you honored the traditions of your parents, but followed the ways of the culture.

The Zealots wanted to rule over the culture. They thought that the huge problems of the world were due to the type of government that was in charge. If you were one of the Zealots, you thought that everything would be better in the world if you were the ones who made the laws and ruled the people.

The Essenes lived separately from the culture. They thought the huge problems of the world were a result of the culture. If you were an Essene, you thought that the best way to not sin was to stay away from sinners.

Jesus thought the huge problems of the world were in the hearts of humans, and the only way to change the world was to change people. So, what's Jesus' plan for changing people's hearts.

***Jesus is different from religious leaders.*** He came to show you how to live. Instead of telling you how to live, he lived it out right in the culture.

Jesus didn't preach at you. Jesus didn't just turn a blind eye to your lifestyle. Jesus didn't try to make laws to rule over you. Jesus didn't try to live a perfect life on earth in a monastery – as far as he could from you.

Jesus embodied His teachings so you could see how to love. He said, *"I've laid down a pattern for you. What I've done, you do."* (John 13:15 Message)

Jesus practiced his own teachings. In fact, Jesus taught you that it won't make sense to you until you start to live it out:

*"Anyone who listens to my teaching and follows it is wise, like a person who builds a house on solid rock." (Matthew 7:24 NLT)*

Jesus even goes so far as saying that those who hear the teachings but don't live them out are foolish.

*"But if you just use my words for Bible studies and don't work them into your life, you are like a stupid carpenter..." (Matthew 7:26 Message)*

What bothered Jesus the most was religious leaders who didn't practice what they taught.

*So, practice and obey whatever they tell you, but don't follow their example. For they don't practice what they teach. (Matthew 23:3 NLT)*

**Jesus is different from religious leaders.** He died for you. A question that may pop into your head when you hear this is: Why? It's not that you don't appreciate someone dying for you; you just wonder why they have to go through all of that.

Not only did Jesus come to show you how to live, but he died to pay for the consequences of our innate self-centered nature.

The Bible teaches that you were born into a world that is not perfect (no kidding!) and that it's not perfect because the people in it are not perfect. Everyone does things that they should not and doesn't do things that they should. Everyone misses the mark and the Bible calls this sin (an old archery term for missing the target). *"For everyone has sinned; we all fall short of God's glorious standard." (Romans 3:23 NLT)*

Because you and I share the same world, our actions have consequences. What I do affects you. What I don't do affects you. And the other way around.

This is magnified because you and I are not the only people alive. Billions of people share the same world and that's just today. Even more have shared the same world since the beginning of time as we know it.

Everyone's sin hurts other people and all of us have been hurt by the sins of people from the very beginning.

The Bible tells you that Adam and Eve chose to sin. Their sin hurt them, it hurt the heart of God, and it hurts you and me. It hurt everyone. And this cycle continues from generation to generation. This is known as "the Fall." And the consequence of the Fall is death – *"For the wages of sin is death, but the free gift of God is eternal life through Christ Jesus our Lord." (Romans 6:23 NLT)*

Jesus came to pay for everyone's sin and everyone's consequences. Religious leaders can try to live perfect lives (and nobody can really do it), but can they pay for everyone's sins? Who can pay for all of the sins of all of the human beings that have ever lived?

It would take someone who could live a perfect life because then they would not deserve the death penalty. But it would take more than that. This innocent person would then need to take everybody's death penalty on themselves. So, just as one person (Adam) brought sin and its consequences into the world, one person (Jesus) would take it out.

*If one man's sin put crowds of people at a dead-end abyss of separation from God, just think what God's gift poured through one man, Jesus Christ, will do! There's no comparison between that death-dealing sin and this generous, life-giving gift. (Romans 5:15 Message)*

Jesus told his apprentices that he was going to do this: *From then on Jesus began to tell his disciples plainly that it was necessary for him to go to Jerusalem...he would be killed, but on the third day he would be raised from the dead.". Matthew 16:21 (NLT)*

Jesus is different from religious leaders because he died in your place. The religious leaders are the ones who wanted to kill him. But Jesus did not stay dead.

**Jesus is different from religious leaders.** He rose from the dead to give us life forever. *"...since I live, you also will live." John 14:19 (NLT)*

Jesus is different from religious leaders because he didn't come to improve our lives, He came to make you come alive.

*Jesus told him, "I am the way, the truth, and the life. No one can come to the Father except through me.". John 14:6 (NLT)*

Religious leaders cannot give you life – they can only give you rules. Jesus gives life. And Jesus brings life to the culture. This is why Jesus is different than the religious leaders.

## The Big Idea:
Jesus is different than religious leaders.

## Question:
What do you believe about Jesus?

## Think about Jesus' words
*...I am the way, the truth, and the life. No one can come to the Father except through me. (John 14:6 NLT)*

## Day 17
# Jesus moves into the Neighborhood

### Jesus moves into the Neighborhood
*The Word became flesh and blood and moved into the neighborhood. John 1:14 (Message)*

Jesus moves into the neighborhood. Why? Because you can't change the world without living in it. That's why Jesus came. That is why God put on a human body and died on the cross. There was no other way. Imagine that – God becoming a human being to put the world right and to show you who He is and how to live in his world.

*The Word became flesh and blood and moved into the neighborhood. (John 1:14)*

When Jesus came into the world there were two very separate kingdoms. There was the Kingdom of Rome that spread out over the earth and offered people every pleasure in the world. And there was the Kingdom of Religion that attempted to protect the people of God from the evils of the Kingdom of Rome.

If you lived in the Kingdom of Rome, your goal was to be happy by going after everything you want. The religious leaders thought you were pagans (godless) and you thought the religious leaders were strange.

If you lived in the Kingdom of Religion, your goal was to keep all the rules. And you were concerned about the values of the Kingdom of Rome creeping into the lives of your people.

To stop this, you create a bubble for you and your people to live in. The bubble is sort of your own private world away from the world where you can interact with religious people without the worry of you or your loved ones being pulled into the pagan culture.

In the bubble, you recreate everything that is outside of the bubble so that you never have to go outside of it. Those who live in "the bubble" think that the way to not sin is to stay away from sinners. So, you stay away.

The upside to the bubble is that there are a lot of other people like you that you can meet and talk to about how bad the world is getting.

The downside to the bubble is that the world never gets any better, and you live in this false sense of security that you and your loved ones are safe from the pagan culture. And…you miss out on a lot of really good opportunities to change the world as you live inside the bubble.

Every once in a while, you emerge from the bubble to remind the people outside the bubble how bad they are and how they could become better if they lived in the bubble with you.

"Hey, you bad people out there! You need God! We've got him here in the bubble with us. Come get in our bubble so you can get God in your life and be free like us!"

Though you see people outside the bubble all the time, every once in a while, you have to interact with them. You aren't quite sure what to say and it's pretty awkward. You just don't have anything in common.

At the end of the week, you gather with the rest of your friends from the bubble and talk about how bad the world is and how much people need God.

Then one day, an "outsider" from the culture enters your bubble. Heads turn. Eyes open wide. Mouths open even wider. Who is this outsider? And how did they get in here?

You don't understand them and they don't understand you. Your life is just so different. And this is different from what Jesus does.

God put on flesh and blood so he could understand us. Jesus worked a trade so his life would not be different from the apprentices that went on the mission with him.

What made Jesus better at changing the culture was that he lived in it. *"...he had to enter into every detail of human life."* *(Hebrews 2:17 Message)*

Jesus doesn't live in the religious bubble and he doesn't want you to live there either.

***Jesus moved into the neighborhood.*** God wants us to know him. Jesus does not just tell you about God, he is God...in the flesh. This is called the incarnation – fully God, fully human.

*"...We saw the glory with our own eyes. The one of a kind glory – like Father, like son, generous inside and out, true from start to finish." (John 1:14 Message)*

Maybe you have had different ideas about what God is like. Perhaps you see God as an angry judge punishing people for the huge problems in the world. Or maybe you see God as a distant father...someone who brought you into the world but has very little to do with your life.

Jesus shows you that God is not mad at you – he loves you. He's not distant, but nearby. Jesus proved this when he moved into your neighborhood. And you can know him.

*"His purpose was for the nations to seek after God and perhaps feel their way toward him and find him – though he is not far from any one of us. (Acts 17:27 NLT)*

Jesus showed us what God looks like, and neither the Romans nor the religious leaders recognized him.

*He came into the very world he created, but the world didn't recognize him. He came to his own people, and even they rejected him. (John 1:10-11 NLT)*

Think about this: religious leaders spent their whole life studying about God and had no idea who he really was. Jesus put himself in a place where he could be rejected and was rejected. He was abandoned. He was betrayed. And He was crucified. Jesus left his "comfort zone" in heaven for you.

***Jesus moved into the neighborhood.*** God chose his apprentices from the culture. Jesus did not try to find 12 religious leaders to go on a mission with him to change the world. They couldn't. They lived in the bubble.

The apprentices Jesus chose were everyday people who lived in the culture. They were fisherman, tax collectors, zealots, and other unlikely apprentices for a spiritual leader.

He chose people like you. Why? Two reasons: 1) They didn't think that they already knew everything; 2) They knew the people that Jesus wanted to reach. The unlikely apprentice is the most likely person that God uses.

So, Jesus moves into your neighborhood, and knocks on your door. You open it. You let him in. You eat a meal together and become friends. But he doesn't stay. There are other neighborhoods to move into, and he asks you to go with him.

## The Big Idea:
Jesus moves into the neighborhood.

## Question:
What do the people in your life think God looks like?

## Think about Jesus' words
*"The Word became flesh and blood and moved into the neighborhood." (John 1:14 Message)*

## Day 18
# The Culture is not the Enemy

### Jesus responds to criticism that he spends time with "sinners"

*Jesus heard about it and spoke up, "Who needs a doctor: the healthy or the sick? I'm here inviting outsiders, not insiders — an invitation to a changed life, changed inside and out.*
*Luke 5:31-32 (Message)*

The culture is not the enemy. Jesus loves the world. But to those in the religious bubble, the culture represents everything that is bad. They confuse the sins of the culture with the people of the culture.

Although the motto of the bubble is: Love the sinner and hate the sin. In reality, it's more like: Hate the sin and stay away from the sinners.

It's one of the first things you learn in the bubble. As soon as you enter the religious bubble, you are taught to cut off all of your non-bubble friends. People say things like — you become like the people you hang around with. The sad thing is that it is true — over time you become more and more religious and less and less like Jesus.

The culture is not the enemy. The enemy of Jesus is death, and death is caused by sin. The root of sin is self-centered choices--not choosing to love. The middle letter in the word sin is "I". Sin is selfish. The three main sins in the Bible are lust, pride, and greed. All three are focused on self.

There are plenty of examples in the culture of lust, pride, and greed. Jesus came to change this. But there are also plenty of examples of lust, pride, and greed in the bubble. This hypocrisy is what upset Jesus the most.

Jesus' mission was not to build a huge bubble to save people from the world. He came to save the world. He came to change people's hearts. Instead of being disgusted by their broken lifestyles, he accepted people, ate with them in their homes, and loved them so much that they wanted to be with him and become like him.

**The culture is not the enemy.** The enemies of Jesus are those who keep people from entering God's Kingdom.

*I've had it with you! You're hopeless, you religion scholars, you Pharisees! Frauds! Your lives are roadblocks to God's Kingdom. You refuse to enter, and you won't let anyone else in either." (Matthew 23:13 Message)*

It is possible for religious leaders to actually keep ordinary people away from God. Can you believe it? Is it possible that Jesus thought there were people who were so called "God-lovers" that were actually working against the mission?

*"This is war, and there is no neutral ground. If you're not on my side, you're the enemy; if you're not helping, you're making things worse." (Matthew 12:30 Message)*

So, whose side are you on? The test is not what people in the religious bubble think about you. The test is what people outside of the bubble think about you.

If you are on the mission with Jesus, the people in the Kingdom of Rome will know that you are different, but they will actually like you. If you are on the mission with Jesus, the religious leaders will accuse you of not being spiritual enough because of who you keep company with.

*Jesus heard about it and spoke up, "Who needs a doctor: the healthy or the sick? I'm here inviting outsiders, not insiders — an invitation to a changed life, changed inside and out. (Luke 5:31-32 Message)*

Jesus was born an outsider (born to an unwed teenage mother in a shed). Jesus grew up an outsider (he was from the unimportant village of Nazareth). Jesus died an outsider (taken outside the city to be crucified like a criminal on a Roman cross). Jesus loves people outside the bubble, because they are the closest to having their hearts changed. They're the only ones who think that they need God.

Jesus tells the story about two people who come into the temple to pray to God — one a religious leader and the other a tax collector. The religious leader comes to the very front of the temple and says, *"Oh, God thank you that I am not like other people — robbers, crooks, adulterers, or, God forbid, like this tax man. I fast twice a week and tithe on all my income." (Luke 18:12 Message)*

The tax collector comes into the temple but stands in the back. With his face in his hands he says, *"God give mercy. Forgive me a sinner." (Luke 18:13 Message)*

Guess which one Jesus said went home embraced by God? It was the tax man. He got grace. The religious leader didn't get it. And as long as you think that the culture is the enemy, you won't get it either.

*"...for those who exalt themselves will be humbled, and those who humble themselves will be exalted." (Luke 18:14 NLT)*

Jesus changes the culture without participating in the sins of the culture. He knows the culture is not the enemy.

## The Big Idea:
The culture is not the enemy.

## Question:
What do the people who live outside of the religious bubble think about you?

## Think about Jesus' words
*"This is war, and there is no neutral ground. If you're not on my side, you're the enemy; if you're not helping, you're making things worse." Matthew 12:30 (Message)*

## Day 19
# Jesus opens up your heart

### Jesus sends out His apprentices
*Look, I am sending you out as sheep among wolves. So be as shrewd as snakes and harmless as doves.*
*Matthew 10:16 (NLT)*

Jesus accepts you just as you are. Does he approve of everything you do? What do you think? You probably don't even approve of everything you do!

Acceptance and approval – where do you draw the line? What if you accept people in the Kingdom of Rome and they don't change? What if you accept them and they confuse this with approval? Do you want them to think that you approve of the sin in the culture – or in their lifestyle?

Being on the mission with Jesus is a lot tougher than living in the religious bubble or just going with the flow in the Kingdom of Rome. It is a "narrow road."

The Kingdom of Rome draws the line on the side of tolerance. Everyone is accepted and every behavior that is not breaking the law is allowed. The theme is Rome's version of grace.

In the Kingdom of Religion, the line is drawn on the side of the rules. Only the rule keepers are accepted and only what is within the religious law was approved. The theme is Religion's version of truth.

In the Kingdom of God, Jesus draws the line differently. He

draws it at truth _and_ grace. Jesus accepts people as is. Jesus speaks truth about people's hearts. His theme is truth and grace.

_"And the Word became flesh and dwelt among us, and we have seen his glory, glory as of the only Son from the Father, full of grace and truth." (John 1:14 ESV)_

I don't know if you've ever driven over a bridge, but can you imagine driving over a bridge without rails? You're in your car speeding down the highway when the land to the side of the road drops hundreds of feet. Traffic slows to a crawl, as cars hug the yellow line narrowly avoiding each other.

Without the rails people would drive off the road and drive into others. And there is a considerable amount of road rage with people who want to go faster battling those who want everyone to just obey the rules.

The rails on the mission with Jesus are grace and truth. The culture approved of Jesus' lifestyle. They liked him and they respected him. By going on the mission with Jesus you learn how to be full of grace and truth in action.

So…you and the other apprentices are on your way back to the "mission base" with Jesus, and he leads you right through a neighborhood that most of your people avoid. The place is Samaria. The reason why you avoid this place is because there are a lot of Samaritans there (imagine that!).

In the minds of the religious leaders, these are the people who have left the bubble and embraced the sins of the culture. Instead of avoiding this neighborhood like most of your people, Jesus walks right through it – deliberately.

You and your friends are getting hungry and you talk Jesus

into stopping so you can hit the local Costco. While the apprentices go shopping, Jesus hangs out at the water well. It's the middle of the day.

When you come out of the store, Jesus is talking with someone you and your people would never talk to – a Samaritan. And not just a Samaritan, a woman. No man in your culture would stoop to that level – ever!

What you find out is this: the woman was at the well to get water at the same time Jesus was waiting for you in the store. This is odd, because this was always part of a morning routine. Why is she there in the middle of the day? You know why. And so does Jesus. She's trying to avoid the others in the town who draw water from the well.

Jesus does not avoid her and does not avoid talking to her. By asking her for a drink of her water from her pail he both shocks her and shows her that he accepts her. This grace opens the door to a conversation.

When Jesus asks her to come back with her husband, she tries to skirt the issue, but Jesus tells her the truth.

*...Jesus said, "You're right! You don't have a husband – for you have had five husbands, and you aren't even married to the man you're living with now." John 4:17-18 (NLT)*

Jesus reads her mail. So, she tries to turn it into a religious debate of which site is the most spiritual place to worship. Jesus tells her it isn't where you worship but who you are that God looks at.

*"It's who you are and the way you live that count before God...the Father is looking for: those who are simply and honestly themselves before Him in worship." (John 4:23 Message)*

How does she respond? She becomes an apprentice of Jesus—like you-- telling her encounter story of Jesus with others and living out a new life with a changed heart.

*"Many of the Samaritans from the village committed themselves to him because of this woman's witness..." (John 4:39 Message)*

After seeing all of this life-change, you feel a bit sheepish because when you and the apprentices came out of the store; you were offended that Jesus was talking to her.

*"Just then his disciples came back. They were shocked." (John 4:27 Message)*

Can you imagine what you would have done in Jesus' shoes? Would you have avoided her? Ignored her? Judged her? Can you imagine Jesus telling you the truth about your life? How does Jesus get away with so much truth? Answer: grace.

Grace – Jesus accepts you. Truth – Jesus speaks to you about the sins of your heart. By accepting you, Jesus opens your heart up to God.

## The Big Idea:
Jesus opens up people's hearts.

## Question:
How do you live out truth and grace in your world?

## Think about Jesus' words
*"And the Word became flesh and dwelt among us, and we have seen his glory, glory as of the only Son from the Father, full of grace and truth."* (John 1:14 ESV)

## Day 20

# Jesus brings out the best in people

### Salt and light

*You're here to be salt-seasoning that brings out the God-flavors of this earth... You're here to be light, bringing out the God-colors in the World. Matthew 5:13-14 (Message)*

Jesus brings out the best in you. In the same way that salt brings out flavors and light brings out colors in this world, Jesus brings out the best in people.

You know this because he brings out the best in you. By being around Jesus, you become more Godly. By being around Jesus, the people in the culture want to become more Godly.

Nobody in the culture looked at the religious leaders and wanted to be more religious. The people in the culture didn't like them. If people don't like you, they will not want to be like you.

***You are the salt of the earth.*** People liked Jesus just like people like salt. Salt brings out flavor, and Jesus helped them become the person that they always wanted to be but didn't think was possible.

Salt sticks out. And people on the mission with Jesus stick out. You don't stick out because of rule keeping. You stick out because of your heart.

You work differently. You have a great attitude. You work hard as if God was your real boss, because he is. You're honest. You work a full day and you don't lie or cheat. You care about the people you work with and you encourage them. You bring out the best in your company and every team that you're on does better.

You love differently. You have great friendships. You are loyal. You don't gossip. You don't slander. You bring out the best in your friends, and they have a lot more success because of it.

Your family is different. You like each other. You serve each other. Your family has heart.

**You are the salt of the earth.** But salt must be sprinkled out to bring out flavor. Nobody wants a spoonful of salt. And in the same way, nobody looks at a bunch of salt that is stuck together – isolated from the culture – and thinks, "Whatever they have, I need."

Jesus sends you out into the culture so that you are continually reminded that the mission is not about you. And you make people want to love God.

*"in the same way, let your good deeds shine out for all to see, so that everyone will praise your heavenly Father." (Matthew 5:16 NIV)*

**You are the salt of the earth.** But Jesus tells you that it is possible to lose your ability to bring out the best in others.

*"…If you lose your saltiness, how will people taste godliness. You've lost your usefulness and end up in the garbage." (Matthew 5:13 Message)*

How do you lose your saltiness?

On the mission with Jesus, you no longer ask, "Is this wrong?" You ask, "Is this wise? Will this bring the people around me closer to God or drive them further away?"

You lose your saltiness when you get off the mission and you begin to think in terms of yourself – "what's in this for me?" Pride, greed, and lust tempt you to make yourself the center of the story.

*"Stay alert, be in prayer so that you don't wander into temptation without even knowing you are in danger." (Matthew 26:41 Message)*

You don't realize it, but other apprentices are tempted, too. Jesus understands temptation. Everyone on the mission gets tempted to lose their saltiness. It's usually when they lose their connection in prayer with their Father in Heaven.

You don't realize it, but Jesus knows that one of the apprentices will betray him. One will deny him. All will scatter. But that doesn't stop Jesus. He knows that even though they fall down, he is going to rise up. And even after your greatest failure, Jesus is still bringing out your best.

Jesus brings out the best in people and you know this because he brings out the best in you.

## The Big Idea:
Jesus brings out the best in people.

## Question:
How can you bring out the best in
the people around you?

## Think about Jesus' words
*You're here to be salt-seasoning that brings out the God-flavors
of this earth...You're here to be light, bringing out the God-
colors in the World. Matthew 5:13-14 (Message)*

## Week Five
# Practice #4: Jesus apprentices serve the world

### Jesus tells his apprentices who is the greatest

*...whoever wants to become great must become a servant... that is what the Son of Man has done: He came to serve, not be served — and then to give away his life in exchange for the many who are held hostage. Matthew 20:26, 28 (Message)*

# Introduction
# Week Five

What does a great person look like to you? Who do you think is great? Is it a successful business person? A great artist? A famous actor? An all-star athlete? A beautiful model? A powerful politician? A king? A queen?

Most people want to be someone important – someone great. That's why most people like to be served, because it makes them feel bigger. But actually, Jesus thinks that the greatest people are servants, because they impact the largest circle of people.

He says that you become great by serving and asking for nothing in return. Most people don't like to serve, because they don't like doing something without getting something in return. This is why Jesus has to change people's hearts to change the world

Changing the world takes servants, lots of them.

Are you a servant? Following Jesus means serving the world. When you serve, people's hearts will begin to change – starting with yours.

## Day 21
# Serve Jesus by serving the World

### Jesus teaches his apprentices how to serve Him

*Whenever you did one of these things to someone overlooked or ignored, that was me – you did it to me.*
*Matthew 25:40 (Message)*

You serve Jesus by serving the world. This is what Jesus taught his apprentices. How do you know if you serve Jesus? Just ask the people around you – they will tell you if you are a servant or not.

People thought Jesus was a servant because he helped them and didn't ask them to pay for it. That's why the crowds followed him everywhere. He taught. He healed. He changed lives. He changed hearts. He served the world, at no charge. He didn't try to get – he gave. There were huge problems in the world and Jesus changed people's lives by serving. This is what Jesus modeled for his apprentices. So, why did they have such a hard time figuring this out?

Well, serving Jesus seemed a lot more impressive than serving people in the world. Serving them almost makes you feel like…a servant. You didn't mind people thinking you serve Jesus – he was popular and important. But you didn't want anyone to think that you served people who were not as important as you. Jesus taught that the more important you want to be, the more you served others.

*"Whoever wants to become great must become a servant. Whoever wants to be first among you must be your slave." (Matthew 20:26-27 Message)*

Jesus' apprentices liked the idea of serving Jesus, He was amazing! They probably didn't even mind serving the crowds – they got a lot of attention for this. But the last thing they would want to do is serve each other.

Serving each other was a little bit harder because they were always comparing themselves to each other.

*"They started arguing over which of them would be the most famous." (Luke 9:46 Message)*

Although it is hard to serve when your service is taken for granted, the true test of a servant is how you respond when someone treats you like one.

Do you want to be famous in this life or great in God's Kingdom forever? Are there people that you are willing to serve and some you aren't?

Jesus separates his true apprentices by those who serve and those who don't. Jesus tells a story to describe this. Jesus calls the servants sheep and the ones who don't serve goats.

*"…he will sort the people out, much as a shepherd sorts out sheep and goats…" (Matthew 25:32 Message)*

The moment you become a Jesus apprentice, you become a servant to the world.

**Jesus makes you into a servant by changing the way you look at people.** The apprentices had an unspoken rating system on who should get help and who shouldn't. Do you? Jesus apprentices (the sheep) don't. They see that they are serving Jesus every time they serve other people.

*"Then the King will say, 'I'm telling you the solemn truth: Whenever*

103

*you did one of these things to someone overlooked or ignored, that was me – you did it to me." (Matthew 25:40 Message)*

Jesus tells you that whenever you serve someone in the world who is overlooked or ignored, without realizing it, you are serving him.

*"Then those 'sheep' are going to say, "Master, what are you talking about? When…?" (Matthew 25:37 Message)*

**Jesus makes you into a servant by changing the way you look at your schedule.** Serving is not just when you have time for it, but when the need is there. Because the need can't wait.

*"I was hungry and you fed me. I was thirsty and you gave me something to drink. I was homeless and you gave me a room. I was shivering and you gave me clothes. I was sick and you stopped in to visit me. I was in prison and you came to me." (Matthew 25:36 Message)*

Some people think that the way to get closer to Jesus is to not do certain things. But Jesus teaches you that the best way to get closer to Him is to actually do something – serve. The reward of serving is that you get closer to God.

*"…Enter, you who are blessed by my Father! Take what's coming to you in this Kingdom." (Matthew 25:34 NIV)*

How you serve here on earth will determine how much God entrusts you with in eternity. Your reward for helping people will last forever.

Some people may not thank you. Some people may not even notice you. But God notices. And he says: well done. *"Enter, you who are blessed by my Father!" (Matthew 25:34 Message)*

These are the words that every apprentice wants to hear.

## The Big Idea:
You serve Jesus by serving the world.

## Question:
How can you serve the world today?

## Think about Jesus' words
*Whenever you did one of these things to someone overlooked or ignored, that was me — you did it to me.*
*Matthew 25:40 (Message)*

## Day 22

# Jesus' servants are the happiest people

### Jesus is tempted by Satan with the kingdoms of the world

*Worship the Lord your God and only him. Serve him with absolute single-heartedness. Matthew 4:10 (Message)*

Jesus' servants are the happiest people. Why? Is it because they get to see the smile and joy on someone's face? Sometimes that happens, but that's not why they are the happiest. They are the happiest because they know their life is making a difference. Isn't that when you are happiest? Jesus sets you free from selfish living to serve others and bring the good life of God's Kingdom to someone else.

Some people are great at making you laugh so you forget about your problems for a while. Others can help you drink your problems away at least until the morning after. You can pay good money for someone to lift you out of your depression, but in the end your problems still exist and so do the huge problems of the world.

The great temptation in life is to focus on what you think will make you happy. This is why the religious leaders lived to impress others and why the people in the Kingdom of Rome searched for fulfillment in new relationships, new toys, new houses, and new adventures.

Where do you search for happiness? Maybe a better question is where are you tempted to make it all about yourself? Each temptation is an opportunity for you to show that you are one of Jesus' servants to the world.

Jesus was tempted to make it all about himself. Before Jesus went public with his calling to announce the Kingdom of God, he spent 40 days alone in the desert without eating and was tempted there by the devil. Can you imagine being tempted by the devil after 40 days alone in the desert – starving?

*"The tempter came to him and said, "If you are the Son of God, tell these stones to become bread." (Matthew 4:3 Message)*

The first thing the devil does is tempt Jesus to turn a stone into bread. Don't you think you would have been tempted? I think I would have been tempted to turn the stone into steak and lobster!

Often, temptations are tests where we choose what we think will bring happiness. Jesus chose to trust God with his needs instead of meeting them his own way.

Are you tempted to meet your own needs your own way? Are you wrapped up in trying to make sure that you "get yours"? Jesus frees Himself up to serve, by trusting his Father to serve him.

*"It takes more than bread to stay alive. It takes a steady stream of words from God's mouth." (Matthew 4:4 Message)*

Jesus says God takes care of his servants needs.

*"Seek the Kingdom of God above all else and live righteously and he will give you everything you need." (Matthew 6:33 NLT)*

Another reason that Jesus' servants are the happiest people is that they have learned to be content with who they are.

They don't feel that they have to look like a big shot.

*"For the second test the Devil took him to the Holy City. He sat him on top of the Temple and said, "Since you are God's son, jump." (Matthew 4:5-6 Message)*

The Temple was center of the attention in the community. Everyone who was anyone was there. This was the Hollywood of the religious world. The devil tempts Jesus to show off; prove to everyone who he is. Do you feel like you have to prove yourself? Are you tempted to show off? You can't try to impress people and also be a servant.

*"Do you want to stand out. Then step down. Be a servant. If you puff yourself up, you'll get the wind knocked out of you. But if you are content to simply be yourself, your life will count for plenty." (Matthew 23:11-12 Message)*

Happiness isn't found in trying to make yourself better than other people. It's found in being you.

The religious leaders couldn't be servants because they were trying to impress. Jesus was comfortable with serving because he was comfortable with who he was.

Jesus' servants are comfortable with who they are and content with what they have.

Are you content with what you have? You won't be a servant until you're content. Why? Because until you're content, you'll always want more. And as long as you want more, you are not free to serve. You will never have enough.

Jesus was then tempted to become the ruler of all the kingdoms of the world.

*"Next the devil took him to the peak of a very high mountain and*

*showed him all the kingdoms of the world and their glory. "I will give it all to you," he said, "if you will kneel down and worship me."'* (Matthew 4:8-9 NLT)

Jesus refused to make that deal with the devil. What would you have done? What if you knew that the other alternative ended in death? Jesus refused the kingdoms of the world because the mission he was on was worth much more. And you can't say no to temptation if you don't have something better to say yes to.

Jesus knew that all of the kingdoms of this world wouldn't satisfy him…because he'd end up all alone. Would it be worth it to you to be rich and famous and powerful and end up unloved and alone?  Happiness is something that people in the Kingdom of Rome chase but never actually get.

If you don't serve others, eventually you slip into thinking that your problems are bigger than the huge problems of the world. This would make anyone melancholy.  So, doesn't it make sense that if you are down the thing to do is to start serving others? Do something to put a smile on someone else's face and see what happens.

Jesus' servants are the happiest people in the world. And if you become one of his servants you will be happy, too.

### The Big Idea:
Jesus' servants are the happiest people.

### Question:
What can you do today to bring happiness to someone else?

### Think about Jesus' words
*Worship the Lord your God and only him. Serve him with absolute single-heartedness.*
*Matthew 4:10 (Message)*

## Day 23
# Small acts change the world

### Jesus tells us where to start

*This is a large work I've called you into, but don't be overwhelmed by it. It's best to start small. Give a cool cup of water to someone who is thirsty... the smallest act of giving or receiving makes you a true apprentice.*
*Matthew 10:42 (Message)*

Small acts change the world. Or do they? The problems of the world are huge. So, doesn't it make more sense to say that huge acts change the world? Maybe, but that is not what Jesus taught his apprentices.

When you hear that the world needs help to solve huge problems, are you inspired or overwhelmed? Maybe a little of both, but probably more overwhelmed. It's not that you don't want to solve the huge problems of the world, but you have your own problems to deal with. What you'd really like to figure out is how to get through the month with some money left in the bank or how to get through the day without blowing up at someone. What you really want is a break from "your" problems, not more of them. You're simply trying to make it to the weekend!

However, that's not living---it's surviving. You were created to be alive – to live the good life – to give the good life to others – Jesus' Life. Relax...you don't have to change the world alone. When Jesus invites you into his life and shows you God's Kingdom, he also invites you to change the world with him and his apprentices. Whether you realize it or not, Jesus is still changing the world through the hearts of his apprentices who live by his words and are empowered by his Spirit. Jesus' plan for changing people's hearts is not by a few followers doing huge acts but all of his followers doing small acts.

*This is a large work I've called you into, but don't be overwhelmed by it. It's best to start small. Give a cool cup of water to someone who is thirsty…the smallest act of giving or receiving makes you a true apprentice. Matthew 10:42 (Message)*

Jesus asks you to do what you can do – not what you can't do.

**Small acts change the world.** Jesus' servants give people a cool cup of water. Does that sound like something you can do? Sure, you can do it. But does that mean God's plan to change the world by changing people's hearts includes millions of apprentices handing out water bottles. Perhaps…if that is what the person in front of you needs.

Everyone is thirsty. But not everyone is thirsty for the same thing. Some thirst for water, while others thirst for attention. Think about it. Who are some people in your world that are thirsty for attention? Is it a teenage son of a friend who looks over at the sidelines after a goal to see if anyone who cares about him saw it? Is it an elderly woman in a nursing home who stares at the door of her room hoping today one of her family members will visit her, but nobody comes…for months? Is it the single mom, who sits alone every other weekend when the kids are at her ex's? Who are the thirsty in your world? What is a cold cup of water for them?

What if one of the small acts you did every day was to give people attention? This is hard to do when the first thoughts of your day are about you. One of the practical ways to prepare yourself for this is by giving God your attention. For a few moments in the morning, focus your attention on God. Throughout the day, think about him. The Bible calls this worship. When you get close to God, he gets close to you, and his love flows through you to others.

The most practical thing Jesus could do as an example of the power of small acts was to wash someone's feet. And this is a job that you would not want!

In Jesus' day, people walked everywhere just like you did before you got your driver's license (assuming you have one). The roads were dusty and regardless of if you had the money for sandals or not, your feet got really dirty. So, washing your feet was pretty important...and also pretty gross.

You loved to go to the houses with servants, because part of a servant's job was to wash guests' feet. If you knew someone who had a servant, you went to their house all the time.

The night Jesus was betrayed and arrested – the night of the Last Supper, Jesus washed his apprentices' feet.

*"...and poured water into a basin. Then he began to wash the disciples' feet, drying them with the towel he had around him." (John 13:5 NLT)*

Think about the greatest person in the world coming to where you are right now – and washing your car? Or shining your shoes? Or rubbing your feet? For free!

Jesus is showing you the way to people's hearts is through meeting their needs. Jesus' small act of washing his apprentices' feet changed their hearts and has changed millions of hearts since. Why? It wasn't because of the apprentices' clean feet. It was because he showed them nobody is too good to serve, and nothing is too small to make a difference.

*And since I, your Lord and Teacher, have washed your feet, you ought to wash each other's feet. I have given you an example to follow. Do as I have done for you.". John 13:14-15 (NLT)*

Small acts change the world, because small acts open up people's hearts to change. Small acts are symbolic of the larger things that need to be understood. Love shows up in small acts. Love is practical. You can do it. The culture changes when Jesus' apprentices do the small things. And when all of Jesus' apprentices do small things, the huge problems of the world don't seem so overwhelming.

## The Big Idea:
Small acts change the world.

## Question:
Who are some people that you can give
your attention to today?

## Think about Jesus' words
*This is a large work I've called you into, but don't be
overwhelmed by it. It's best to start small. Give a cool cup of
water to someone who is thirsty… the smallest act of giving or
receiving makes you a true apprentice.
Matthew 10:41-42 (Message)*

## Day 24

# Are you too busy to help heal the world?

### Follow Jesus and serve with Him

*If any of you wants to serve me, then follow me. Then you'll be where I am, ready to serve at a moment's notice.*
*John 12:26 (Message)*

Are you too busy to help heal the world? Jesus isn't. Being a servant to the world is not a part-time job. You never know when you are going to be needed most. Jesus apprentices are always ready.

If you read the story of Jesus in one of the gospels (Matthew, Mark, Luke, or John), one of the things you will notice is that most of Jesus' miracles happened when he was on the way to do something else.

One time Jesus had just finished teaching when a local official came to get Jesus because his daughter died. Jesus and His apprentices get up and go to bring her back to life. On the way there, a woman who had been hemorrhaging for twelve years slips in from the crowd, reaches out, touches his robe, and is healed.

Jesus stops. He says to the healed woman, *"Courage, daughter. You took a risk of faith, and now you're well." (Matthew 9:21 Message)*

Jesus and his apprentices reach the house of the local

official. Jesus goes into the house, takes the girl's hand, and brings her to her feet alive.

As soon as Jesus leaves the house, two blind men are crying out for Jesus, *"...Son of David, have mercy on us!" (Matthew 9:27 NLT)*

Welcome to the world of Jesus – the life of a servant. He has just been interrupted three times in a row in one day. How do you handle interruptions? Depends, right? Depends on how much stuff is going on in your life and who's interrupting.

You can't schedule miracles because the people come to you. Jesus didn't say to the local official – "You know, next Tuesday is really better for me. Can you come back then?" He doesn't say to the bleeding woman – "You know, I really can't be distracted right now. I'm on the way to do something really important."

*Jesus' servants get interrupted.* And you prepare for this by simplifying your life. Jesus freed himself up to be able to do these things. The first thirty years of his life was spent getting everything ready so he could spend the last three giving 100% of himself to his mission.

How do you do this?

*Jesus and his apprentices lived a simple life.* Look at your life. If Jesus sat down with you and your calendar, what would change?

Something has to give. If every time someone comes to you and you wish they would come at a better time, maybe something is not right with your calendar.

Where do you start? Jesus starts with your attitude. In the

Kingdom of Rome, how you spend your time is your business. It's your life. Your time is spent pleasure seeking and trying to be happy. Your calendar is full of all of the entertainment and amusement of the culture. It's also full of all you've got to do to pay for that lifestyle.

In the Kingdom of Religion, the rules and regulations dictate how you spend your time. You could help people as long as it wasn't on a holy day – because that day was for God. Does that sound strange or what? It sure did to Jesus. When you live in the religious bubble, you simply don't have time for people outside the bubble.

In the Kingdom of God, you make time for people because people matter to God. Your attitude is – it's not my life – my life belongs to Jesus. Jesus fills in your calendar and plans out your life. You never know what exciting new adventure Jesus is going to take you on next. The mission is full of surprises. Being on the mission with Jesus means that you're always going to have great stories to tell. Just like his apprentices had great stories to tell.

Jesus didn't do everything. Nobody has more than 24 hours – even the Savior of the World. You can't just add more time to your life. You have to do less. Jesus did more by doing less and so will you.

*"What I'm trying to do here is to get you to relax, to not be so preoccupied with getting, so you can respond to God's giving."* (Matthew 6:31 Message)

What is on your calendar that Jesus would cut out? What is it? It's not sleep. It's not eating. It's not your job (remember Jesus did work as a carpenter for 90% of his life on earth). It's not time with family. What is it?

What is on your calendar that Jesus would cut back because

it is out of balance? It's not gathering with other apprentices. It's not connecting with people who are not yet on the mission. What is it? What's out of balance? Do you feel like you are in a vicious pleasure cycle of new "toys" and experiences to recharge you – only to end up working far too many hours to pay for them?

How do you recharge?

Jesus took time out to recharge. Jesus recharged by praying. *"While it was still night, way before dawn, he got up and went out to a secluded spot and prayed." (Mark 1:35 Message)*

Jesus recharged by getting away. *"Jesus went off with his disciples to the sea to get away." (Mark 3:7 Message)*

If Jesus needed to recharge, you do too. Maybe you get away, but you don't recharge. Have you ever come back from vacation and needed to go to work so you could rest up? What if you vacationed differently? If Jesus was planning your vacation, what would you do? One thing for sure, it would not be a vacation away from the mission.

Jesus recharged by not doing everything himself. Jesus had no problem releasing and empowering others to do stuff. Well before most people would have thought that the apprentices were ready for public service, Jesus sent them out…twice! And when Jesus rises from the dead, instead of filling his schedule with a "Change the World Tour". He leaves!

"Apprentices…it's your turn. I'll give you my words and my spirit." And now instead of 12 apprentices, Jesus can have millions.

If you were to write the adventure of your life with Jesus 20 years from now, what stories would there be? Going on the mission with Jesus and serving people guarantees incredible stories of changed hearts and changed lives. You may be busy now. But you can change that. Because you aren't too busy to change the world.

## The Big Idea:
Are you too busy to help heal the world?

## Question:
If Jesus were in charge of your calendar, what would he change?

## Think about Jesus' words
*If any of you wants to serve me, then follow me. Then you'll be where I am, ready to serve at a moment's notice.*
*John 12:26 (Message)*

## Day 25
# Your dreams were meant to help heal the world

### Jesus teaches the secret to making a difference in the world

*I tell you the truth, unless a kernel of wheat is planted in the soil and dies, it remains alone. But its death will produce many new kernels – a plentiful harvest of new lives.*
John 12:24 (NLT)

Your dreams were meant to help heal the world. Think about it. What did you dream of doing when you were a child? Do you remember? Maybe you do, maybe you don't. Most children dream of doing something noble with their life – like saving people out of fires, helping people get well, or simply leading us into world peace.

If you had one of these desires, is it possible that God put that seed there? God gives you dreams to change the world so he can change you. So how does this work?

Well, your dreams inspire you to be great. Take Simon Peter for example. Simon was probably a lot like you in that he wanted his life to be significant – he wanted to do something important with his life. He probably felt deep down he might be a leader – someone special, but needed to hear someone else say it.

But nobody said it. Simon was not one of those who were selected to be one of his nation's future leaders. He was a commercial fisherman. It's a great job, but it's not necessarily a "change the world" occupation. But Jesus seemed to think that fishermen were the perfect people to do something great. So, Jesus recruited Simon. Simon longed to hear someone say that he could have significance, and that is exactly what happened when Simon met Jesus.

So, imagine you are Simon. Your brother has just seen what he believes is the leader who will change the world – the Messiah. He comes and grabs you saying, "Hey, Simon, you've got to come with me and see this Jesus guy!"

*"Andrew, Simon Peter's brother, was one of the two who heard John's witness and followed Jesus. The first thing he did after finding where Jesus lived was find his own brother, Simon, telling him, "We've found the Messiah" (that is, "Christ"). He immediately led him to Jesus. (John 1:40-41 Message)*

So, you go to meet Jesus and he gives you a nickname.

*Jesus took one look up and said, "You're John's son, Simon? From now on your name is Cephas" (or Peter, which means "Rock"). (John 1:42 Message)*

Jesus sees something in you – the potential to do something great – and changes your name from Simon (meaning "reed") to Peter (meaning "rock"). Jesus gives you a name to live up to and then he calls you to go on the mission.

*"Jesus said to Simon, 'There is nothing to fear. From now on you'll be fishing for men and women.' They pulled their boats up on the beach, left them, nets and all, and followed him." (Luke 5:10-11 Message)*

You leave everything to follow your dream to make a difference with your life. Why? Because Jesus believes in you and it's very powerful to have someone believe in you especially if it's the Savior of the World. So, you follow Jesus and he uses your dreams to begin to change your heart. And a number of significant events shape you.

There's the moment when Jesus is walking on the water to catch up to you and the other apprentices, and you blurt out, *"...Lord, if it's really you, tell me to come to you, walking on the water." (Matthew 14:28 NLT)*

Jesus says to you, *"Come."*

You stand up. You start to put a foot out of the boat and into the water which doesn't seem too bad until you lift the other foot up. All of a sudden you find yourself standing on a lake. Not near, not by, not at, not in – you are standing ON a lake with Jesus.

How cool do you feel about yourself at that moment? Pretty cool...until you notice that there are some pretty big waves coming your way and you start to sink. You shout – *Save me, Lord! (Matthew 14:30 NLT)*

Jesus grabs you and says, *"You have so little faith...why did you doubt me?" (Matthew 14:31 NLT)*

Why did you doubt? Maybe because you had never walked on water before and neither had anyone else in the world not named Jesus? Your dreams of doing something great with your life caused you to do something that you'd never done before. Your dreams got you out of the boat. Sure-you doubted. But you also stepped out.

You step out again when Jesus asks you and the other apprentices who you all think he is. While the others are thinking if they should speak out, you speak up.

*Simon Peter answered, "You are the Messiah, the Son of the Living God." (Matthew 16:16 NLT)*

Jesus responds by saying to you, *"Now I say to you that you are Peter (which means 'rock'), and upon this rock I will build my church, and all the powers of hell will not conquer it." (Matthew 16:18 NLT)*

There it is. Not only do you dream of doing something great with your life, but Jesus has told you that you are going to be foundational to his whole "change the world" movement.

Perfect...right? You dream it. Jesus says it. It's done. End of story. Except, here's the twist: Jesus is betrayed by one of the other apprentices and then crucified on a cross. In the process, you deny that you ever knew him. Jesus dies. And you fail.

"Okay, God...how is this part of the dream?"

Failure...it's God's way of changing you. It's an opportunity for God to work deeper in your heart and character and make your dreams about the mission and not about you. God did not give you a dream so you could become great but so you could make his name great. God did not give you a dream so you could rule the world but so you could change the world. Is it possible that failure in your life is God's way of preparing you for something great?

Jesus put it this way: *"Listen carefully: unless a grain of wheat is buried in the ground, dead to the world, it is never any more than a grain of wheat. But if it is buried, it sprouts and reproduces itself many times over. In the same way, anyone who holds on to life just as it is destroys that life. But if you let it go, reckless in your love, you'll have it forever, real and eternal." (John 12:24-25 Message)*

Once your dream dies, God is able to do a miracle – a resurrection. The dream comes true God's way, in God's time, and he gets all the glory.

When Jesus rose from the dead, he found Peter, and reminded him that he was going to do something great. Jesus gave him a second chance. 50 days later (on the day of Pentecost), Peter preached a message that changed people's hearts and caused 3,000 people to get baptized and go on the mission.

So, where are you? Have your dreams come true? Did they change the world? Did they change you? What is God up to? You can find out by surrendering your dreams to God's leadership. Remember, your dreams were meant to heal the world.

## The Big Idea:
Your dreams were meant to help heal the world.

## Question:
What is God doing in your heart?

## Think about Jesus' words
*I tell you the truth, unless a kernel of wheat is planted in the soil and dies, it remains alone. But its death will produce many new kernels—a plentiful harvest of new lives.*
*John 12:24 (NLT)*

## Week Six
# Practice #5:
# Jesus asks for everything

### The commitment of following Jesus
*So you cannot become my disciple without giving up everything you own. Luke 14:33 (NLT)*

### Jesus apprentices use money to serve God
*No one can serve two masters...you cannot serve God and be enslaved to money. Matthew 6:24 (NLT)*

# Introduction
# Week Six

What do you think it takes to change the world? Is it the right government? Is it the right laws? Is it the right religion? Or is it tolerance in all these things? What does it take to change the world?

Jesus models for his apprentices that it takes every apprentice giving everything they have to change the world. If you think being a servant to the world is tough, try dying for it.

So where do you start? Jesus says that you give your life by first giving your heart. This is why. If you give your heart first, the rest will follow. But if you give everything except your heart, eventually you'll want it all back.

Jesus gave his heart. And then he gave his time, his money, and his life. The most natural human tendency is to want to follow Jesus part way. You think you're only holding back a little bit of your time, your money or…but what you're really holding back is your heart. And you can't follow Jesus without giving him your heart.

Jesus asks for everything.

## Day 26

# It takes a lot to heal the world

### Jesus in the Garden of Gethsemane the night of His arrest

*Father, if you are willing, please take this cup of suffering away from me. Yet I want your will to be done, not mine.*
*Luke 22:42 (NLT)*

### Jesus lays out the cost to change the world

*Simply put, if you're not willing to take what is dearest to you, whether plans or people, and kiss it good-bye, you cannot be my disciple. Luke 14:33 (Message)*

It takes a lot to change the world. Don't you agree? If it were easy to change the world, more people would do it. It takes a lot to change the world, but what does it take a lot of? It seems like Jesus thought it took a lot of commitment from a few people.

During the first year of Jesus' public Change The World Tour, he was very popular. Jesus wasn't trying to get a crowd. He was trying to get away from the crowds. People showed up everywhere he went. Word spread.

*"...he left in a boat to a remote area to be alone. But the crowds heard where he was headed and followed on foot from many towns. Jesus saw the huge crowd as he stepped from the boat, and he had compassion on them and healed their sick." (Matthew 14:13-14 NLT)*

Jesus taught them. He healed their sick. And then he fed them. There were approximately 15,000 people there (5,000 men). And Jesus feeds all these people with a boy's lunch – two fish and five loaves of bread.

You can imagine that this only got the crowds going even more.

*"Jesus saw that in their enthusiasm, they were about to grab him and make him king, so he slipped off..."* (John 6:15 Message)

When night comes, Jesus' apprentices headed back across the water. Jesus catches up with them (well...walks on the water up to them), gets in the boat, and arrives on the other side.

The crowd notices that Jesus and his apprentices are gone, so they all jump in their boats to find them. Finally, they catch up to him and Jesus begins by calling for commitment.

*"You've come looking for me not because you saw God in my actions but because I fed you...for free...throw your lot in with the One that God has sent. That kind of commitment gets you in on God's works."* (John 6:26, 29 Message)

Here is the crowd of people that Jesus fed with the bread and fish and Jesus lays out the commitment by basically asking – do you want me or what I can give you? Listen to their response: *"When we see what's up, we'll commit ourselves."* (John 6:30 Message)

Jesus responds by telling them of his commitment to his apprentices.

*"Every person the Father gives me eventually comes running to me. And once that person is with me, I hold on and I don't let go."* (John 6:37 Message)

Then symbolically, he calls for the very commitment that he is going to give. He uses the symbols of bread and wine; his body and his blood to lay out the commitment that it is going to take to change the world. It is going to take your life.

At this point even some of his apprentices are struggling with this and say to Jesus, *"This is tough teaching to swallow."* *(John 6:60 Message)*

Some apprentices left. *"After this a lot of His apprentices left."* *(John 6:66 Message)*

However, Peter said, *"Master, to whom would we go…we've already committed ourselves…"* *(John 6:68-69 Message)*

And with this Jesus solidifies a core group of people who are committed to the mission.

Jesus lowers the bar of acceptance but raises the bar of commitment. He accepts everyone. He even chooses people who the religious leaders did not pick. But he asks these outsiders to give everything.

*"Simply put, if you're not willing to take what is dearest to you, whether plans or people, and kiss it good-bye, you cannot be my disciple."* *(Luke 14:33 Message)*

The reason Jesus asks his apprentices for this level of commitment is because that is what it takes to change the world. And that is exactly the commitment that Jesus made.

Jesus was in the garden of Gethsemane just moments from when he knew that he would be betrayed by Judas, one of his apprentices. He knew that he would be beaten, whipped, mocked, and crucified.

Overwhelmed with grief, Jesus prayed, *"Father, if you are willing, please take this cup of suffering away from me. Yet I want your will to be done, not mine." (Luke 22:42 NLT)*

Talk about commitment. This is Jesus' last chance to pull out. And he doesn't.

Are you in the crowd or are you one of the committed? Jesus shows you that it takes a lot to change the world. And…it's worth it.

## The Big Idea:
It takes a lot to change the world.

## Question:
Are you in the crowd or a part of
the committed core?

## Think about Jesus' words
*So you cannot become my disciple without giving up everything you own. Luke 14:33 (NLT)*

**Day 27**

# What do you have to give up?

## Jesus and the Rich Young Ruler

*Looking at the man, Jesus felt genuine love for him. "There is still one thing you haven't done," he told him. "Go and sell all your possessions and give the money to the poor, and you will have treasure in heaven. Then come, follow me."*
*Mark 10:21 (NLT)*

What do you have to give up? This isn't a very popular message, but how else do you change the world? It's pretty unrealistic to think that you can have everything in the world and change it at the same time.

Jesus taught his apprentices that the first thing you have to give up is…yourself. That's Jesus' plan. Change the world by changing people's heart starting with your own. In fact, Jesus teaches that by giving yourself up you actually end up with a whole lot more.

*"If you try to hang on to your life, you will lose it. But if you give up your life for my sake and for the sake of the Good News, you will save it." (Mark 8:35 NLT)*

Jesus not only teaches this, he models it. His apprentices get to see it in action.

The very first thing you do when you follow Jesus is you give God yourself - your heart. If you give God your heart, then everything you give after that matters because your love comes with it. If you don't give your heart, then everything you give is wasted – because it's not you!

Jesus said it this way to the religious leaders: *"What sorrow awaits you Pharisees! For you are careful to tithe even the tiniest income from your herb gardens, but you ignore justice and the love of God. You should tithe, yes, but do not neglect the more important things."* (Luke 11:42 NLT)

God wants way more than your money – he wants you. You may look at giving 10% of your income ("tithe") as something to live up to, but Jesus thinks that standard is too low if you give it without your heart.

So, what does Jesus want? Jesus points his apprentices to a widow who gives a few cents in the collection. Her amount is less, but her sacrifice is greater.

*"The truth is that this poor widow gave more to the collection than all the others put together. All the others gave what they'll never miss; she gave extravagantly what she couldn't afford – she gave her all."* (Mark 12:43-44 Message)

Jesus wants your heart and you give your heart when you give what you know you will miss. And the truth is that there is no way to change the world by giving God what you really won't miss. It takes treasures given from your heart to change the world, because that is what it takes to change you.

*"Wherever your treasure is, there the desires of your heart will also be."* (Matthew 6:21 NLT)

While on the mission, Jesus is approached by a rich, young ruler. What a perfect prospect for an apprentice to change the world. He is young. He has resources. He is a leader.

You would probably think this is the perfect person to have on your team.

He asks Jesus how to get eternal life. Jesus answers by asking the young man if he has obeyed all the commandments. Listen in on their conversation:

*"The young man said, 'I've done all that. What's left?'*

*'If you want to give it all you got,' Jesus replied, 'Go sell your possessions; give everything to the poor. All your wealth will then be in heaven. Then come follow me.'"* (Matthew 19:20-21 Message)

The Bible records that the young man went away sad because he had a lot of wealth. Can you imagine being him? Would you be sad, too? You ask Jesus what you need to do to go on this mission and he says...just one thing...give up everything you have.

Is it possible that Jesus asks all his apprentices to give up everything? Does it mean you have to go and sell all your stuff and give it to the poor? Probably not. But maybe...if it would keep you from really following Jesus. Maybe Jesus wants you not to sell all you have...maybe he wants you to keep it so you can use it for the mission. I don't know. What I do know is this: that as long as your heart is still attached to the stuff in this world, you're not ready to go on the mission with Jesus and you're not ready to change the world.

Jesus gave up everything. And you have to give up everything to go with him. Every apprentice gives up everything to follow. It is not a few people giving large gifts to change the world – that only changes a few people. It is every apprentice giving what they'll miss that changes the world, because it changes the people who give.

What is it for you? It's not something you want to give up

anyways – it's got to be a sacrifice. It's something close to your heart. It's probably right at the center of your heart. What do you have to give up to go on the mission?

### The Big Idea:
What do you have to give up?

### Question:
How can you give what is close to your heart for the mission?

### Think about Jesus' words
*Wherever your treasure is, there the desires of your heart will also be. Matthew 6:21 (NLT)*

## Day 28
# What do you have to lose?

### Treasures that Last
*"Don't store up treasures here on earth, where moths eat them and rust destroys them, and where thieves break in and steal. Store your treasures in heaven, where moths and rust cannot destroy, and thieves do not break in and steal."*
*Matthew 6:19-20 (NLT)*

What do you have to lose? Maybe I should ask it this way: what do you have to lose that you aren't going to lose anyway?

You may have an estate plan or a trust so that what you have here doesn't end when you end. But at some point, your treasures will be eaten up. What if you could take what you have here and make it count forever?

Jesus says you can.

*"Don't store up treasures here on earth, where moths eat them and rust destroys them, and where thieves break in and steal. Store your treasures in heaven, where moths and rust cannot destroy, and thieves do not break in and steal." (Matthew 6:19-20 NLT)*

Jesus teaches his apprentices to make their resources count. Life is too precious, too short, and you work too hard to waste your treasures...especially on yourself. So how do you not waste them?

You make your resources count by giving. This is the opposite of what you learn when you live in the Kingdom of Rome. In the Kingdom of Rome, you learn to make your resources count…literally count…by getting. Your treasures make you feel good about yourself, but they don't change the world.

Jesus frees you from thinking that your self-worth comes from your net worth.

*Then he said, "Beware! Guard against every kind of greed. Life is not measured by how much you own." Luke 12:15 (NLT)*

The religious leaders gave religiously. They gave a tithe (10%) of all their earnings. Can you imagine what problems could be solved in the world if everyone did that?

Jesus didn't say the religious leaders were wrong for giving the tithe. He said that it's not enough if your hearts not in it. If you're hearts in it, the tithe is not the standard, it is the minimum. Jesus teaches you to start by giving with your heart.

You make your resources count by saving so you can give more. Jesus wants his apprentices to be wise with their resources.

*"And if you are untrustworthy about worldly wealth, who will trust you with the true riches of heaven?" Luke 16:11 (NLT)*

Why don't people save more? In the Kingdom of Rome and the Kingdom of Religion, people use money to buy status. Your status came from the emblem on your chariot or the logo on your religious robe, so to speak.

Think about how much you could save if you didn't care what people thought about you. Think about how much you could give if you could save. And think about how much you could change the world if you could give more. What if you had the money so when you saw a need you could give right to them?

Saving as a lifestyle gives you the flexibility to meet needs when you see them. Saving turns problems into opportunities to make a difference. Saving allows you to meet the need before the window of opportunity closes.

Jesus apprentices give and Jesus apprentices save wisely so they can make an even greater difference in the world.

You make your resources count by living on less so you can give even more. It costs a lot to live. Especially the way certain people choose to live. What if you choose a different lifestyle so that you had more to give and more to save in your change the world fund?

Jesus teaches that the way to live on less starts with your hearts.

*"What I'm trying to do here is to get you to relax, to not be so preoccupied with getting, so you can respond to God's giving. People who don't know God and the way he works fuss over these things, but you know both God and how He works." (Matthew 6:31-32 Message)*

Advertisers teach you to not be content and to think that you're missing out. Jesus teaches you the opposite.

*"Steep your life in God-reality, God-initiative, God-provisions. Don't worry about missing out. You'll find all your everyday human concerns will be met." (Matthew 6:33 Message)*

Jesus teaches you to take your money and use it to change the world. What do you have to lose? Everyone dies. What you do for yourself gets left behind. There will be no U-Haul behind your hearse. What you invest in others pays off for eternity.

## The Big Idea:
What do you have to lose?

## Question:
What are some practical things you can do to get your money on the mission with Jesus?

## Think about Jesus' words
*"Steep your life in God-reality, God-initiative, God-provisions. Don't worry about missing out. You'll find all your everyday human concerns will be met."*
*Matthew 6:33 (Message)*

## Day 29

# Jesus apprentices don't own anything

### Jesus apprentices use money to serve God

*You can't worship two gods at once…you can't worship God and Money both. Matthew 6:24 (Message)*

Jesus apprentices don't own anything. It's not that they don't have anything…they just don't own it. They manage it. Jesus apprentices think that everything they have belongs to God, and he wants them to use it for the mission of changing the world by changing people's hearts.

So, what do you own? Or maybe a better question is what owns you?

Everything in society pushes you to be an owner. Own your own house. Own your own your car. Own your own career. Own your own life. Sounds like a simple life…but it's not. Because the things in life that you own, usually end up owning you. They take your time, your energy, your passion, your focus, and most of all…they take you.

It's possible to get so tied down with all that you own, that you don't have anything to change the world with. You can't serve people, because you're serving your stuff. Jesus said it this way:

*You can't worship two gods at once…you can't worship God and Money both. (Matthew 6:24 Message)*

Jesus tells his apprentices that it is impossible to serve God by serving the world and also serve money. You can't serve both.

When money is your master your life gets complicated. For some that complication is debt. For others it's stress. For others it's worry. Owning your own life takes a lot out of you. It drains you. Jesus as master leads people out of debt and into a simple life.

*"That is why I tell you not to worry about everyday life..." (Matthew 6:25 NLT)*

How would you like to live a worry-free life? Don't own anything. What would it look like if you didn't own anything? Think about it. Not that you don't have anything, but that what you have was owned by Jesus. What if Jesus owned your house, or your car, or your career...? Think about how free you would be.

When you had a problem with something that you own, by giving Jesus ownership, it becomes Jesus' problem. The beauty of Jesus' simple life and the simple life of the apprentices is that by owning nothing – nothing owned them.

*"Look at the birds, free and unfettered... careless in the care of God." (Matthew 6:26 Message)*

The simple life would give you more time, more energy, and probably a little more life to give to change the world. Wouldn't it be great to actually add hours to your life instead of taking them away? Jesus agrees.

*"Can all your worries add a single moment to your life?" (Matthew 6:27 NLT)*

Imagine having more time every day. What would you do with it? You might have time to take a break and blink.

The simple life would free you from what everyone thinks about you. Instead of worrying about the car you own or the clothes you wear, you would be free to focus on making sure other people have clothes, food, and transportation.

*"And why worry about your clothing? Look at the lilies of the field and how they grow...if God cares so wonderfully for wildflowers that are here today and thrown into the fire tomorrow, he will certainly care for you." (Matthew 6:28, 30 NLT)*

Jesus apprentices don't own anything. They don't have to. And neither do you. God knows what you need.

*"These things dominate the thoughts of unbelievers, but your heavenly Father already knows all your needs. (Matthew 6:32 NLT)*

There are two basic approaches to life. The first is the consumer attitude and it basically says - the world exists for me. You get, you take, and you consume. Your money belongs to you and you use it for your happiness.

So, what's another way to approach life? How about the contributor attitude? It says - The world needs me. You give, you care, and you contribute. Instead of new toys, you look for real needs.

You find significance knowing that your simple life is making a difference in the world.

In the Kingdom of Rome, people live with the consumer attitude. If you live in the Kingdom of Rome, you think that your money belongs to you to use for your personal happiness. If you live in the Kingdom of Religion, you think that 10% of your money is God's and 90% of your money belongs to you to use for your personal happiness.

In the Kingdom of God, Jesus' apprentices think that 100% of the money they have belongs to God and they manage it wisely so they can use it to change lives starting today.

So where do you live? Your money can change the world, but your approach to life has to change first. Jesus apprentices live a simple life – they don't own anything.

## The Big Idea:
Jesus apprentices don't own anything.

## Question:
What would the simple life of a Jesus apprentice look like for you?

## Think about Jesus' words
*"No one can serve two masters...you cannot serve both God and be enslaved to money." Matthew 6:4 (NLT)*

## Day 30
# Start with what you have today

### Jesus apprentices use money to serve God
*"...he called ten servants together, gave them each a sum of money, and instructed them, 'Operate with this until I return.'"*
*Luke 19:13 (Message)*

Start with what you have today. It's easy to think that one day when you have more money and more time you will be able to do more things to change the world. Jesus says that you already have more than enough to start to make a difference right now. A little bit of money in the hands of someone with a huge heart can make a big difference. You have enough money for the small acts that show huge grace to help change people's hearts. You can start today.

Imagine if Jesus came to you and two of your closest friends and said that he would like to give each of you some money so you can do something good in the world. Would that surprise you? Would that surprise your friends? Is Jesus someone who gives money, or someone wants yours? Jesus teaches his apprentices that God gives people money to show them what is in their hearts.

*"...he called ten servants together, gave them each a sum of money, and instructed them, "Operate with this until I return." (Luke 19:13 Message)*

So, you and both of your friends each get a sum of money. It's like winning the lottery...with God's help. You wonder how much God gave you, so you look. Then you look at what your friends got. You're just curious. But then you get mad. One of your friends got twice what you got. What's that all about? Then you ask your other friend and find out that they got five times what you got. That's not fair!

*"He called his servants together and delegated responsibilities. To one he gave five thousand dollars, to another two thousand, to a third one thousand, depending on their abilities." (Matthew 25:15 Message)*

Jesus teaches his apprentices that God gives his servants different amounts of money. The natural human thing to do is to look at the one who got the most and compare that amount with what you have.

God knows that different amounts reveal your heart. The biggest part to giving is getting your eyes off yourself. One of the things that will keep you from giving is comparing what you have to what your friends have. Why? Because you'll always want to have as much or more than they do. And somebody always has more than you.

The different amounts are a test to see what is in our heart. Those who have a lot are tempted to focus on what they have instead of the huge problems in the world. They may even worry that they have too much to lose to give a lot. So, they give only a little. Those who have only a little are tempted to focus on what they don't have instead of the huge problems of the world. They worry that they have too little to give...especially, to make a big difference.

Those who are in the middle are tempted, too. They find it hard to give because then they'll never be like their friends who have a lot. And if they give too much, they may become like their friends who don't seem to have enough.

Jesus apprentices don't compare their money with their friends. They are neither envious nor proud. Why? Because their goal isn't to get stuff…it's to change the world.

The different amounts reveal your ability. God knows that everyone is unique, and some are better at certain things than others. What would not be fair is for God to give people with different abilities same amounts and expect the same returns.

God knows the right amount to give you today for your circumstances and his plans. How does he know? God knows your character. And character is tested in the small things. People who are good with small amounts grow big hearts and have lots of character. And Jesus knows you need both ability and character to change the world.

If your heart and character don't grow with your money, your money won't change the world, it will destroy you. People whose money grows faster than character are destroyed by it. That is not a blessing, it's a curse.

So, what are you doing with Jesus' money? In the story, your two friends take what Jesus gave them and they double it. Now, Jesus has twice the money to use to change the world.

Jesus tells your friends, *"Well done, my good and faithful servant. You have been faithful in handling this small amount, so now I will give you many more responsibilities. Let's celebrate together! (Matthew 25:21 NLT)*

Then Jesus comes to you. What did you do? In the story that Jesus told, the one who was given the least did nothing with it.

*"Master, I know you have high standards and hate careless ways, that you demand the best…I was afraid I might disappoint you…so I found a good hiding place and secured your money. Here it is safe and sound down to the last cent." (Matthew 25:24-25 Message)*

But Jesus doesn't want his apprentices to play it safe with the money He gives them. He wants them to risk it to change the world.

*"The master was furious. That's a terrible way to live! It's criminal to live cautiously like that! ... Take the thousand and give it to the one who risked the most." (Matthew 25:26, 28 Message)*

Your money can change the world but first it has to change you. If you're not willing to give when you have a little, you probably won't be willing when you have a lot. In fact, you'll never think you have a lot. When all Jesus apprentices give when they have a little, the huge problems of the world aren't so big. Start with what you have today.

## The Big Idea:
Start with what you have today.

## Question:
What are some small things that you can do to be faithful with Jesus' money?

## Think about Jesus' words
*"Well done, good and faithful servant! You have been faithful with a few things; I will put you in charge of many things. Come and share your master's happiness!"*
*Matthew 25:23 (NIV)*

## Week Seven
# Practice #6:
# Jesus changes people from the Inside Out

### Jesus changes people from the inside out
*(Jesus) will change your life...turning your old life in for a kingdom life...His baptism...will change you from the inside out. Mark 1:7-8 (Message)*

### Jesus to the religious leaders
*...first wash the inside of the cup and the dish, and then the outside will become clean, too. Matthew 23:26 (NLT)*

# Introduction
# Week Seven

Seems like everyone is trying to change something about themselves. People want to change where they live, how they look, what they do, and who is in their life. People make these changes thinking that this will make their life better.

Are you trying to change something about yourself? Why? What are you hoping you will get from these changes?

Jesus apprentices want to change things, too. But instead of spending their time, money, and energy on changing their circumstances or their appearance, they focus on changing the world by changing people's hearts – starting with their own.

Jesus changes his apprentices from the inside out. The same way Jesus wants to change you. And on the mission with Jesus, you learn what matters most to God and what it really takes for people to change.

## Day 31

# Jesus changes people with aggressive grace

### Jesus to the woman caught in adultery

*"Woman, where are they? Does no one condemn you?...
Neither do I...go on your way. From now on, don't sin."*
*John 8:10-11 (Message)*

Jesus changes people with aggressive grace. Aggressive what? Grace. Perhaps you have never thought of grace as being very aggressive. Maybe in your mind grace is something that waits...waits for someone else to be sorry enough to deserve it. Or maybe it means you just look the other way. But is that grace?

Jesus models for his apprentices this aggressive grace that acts first and gives people what they do not deserve. This grace doesn't look the other way, it looks right at you...changing you from the inside out.

In the Kingdom of Rome, the law was very important. It was a way of keeping peace. Grace was not something that was thrown around (although sometimes it could be bought). It's not wise to overlook people's crimes when you're trying to rule the world.

In the Kingdom of Religion, the religious law was very important. Keeping the religious rules was the only way to be right before God. Life in the religious bubble was guided by these rules to keep you and your people from being corrupted by the culture. Keeping the rules was the way to avoid punishment.

Jesus comes into the world and begins giving people grace before they deserve it. No...before they even ask for it.

Imagine you are on the mission with Jesus 2,000 years ago, he's at the temple, teaching people. *"Swarms of people came to him. He sat down and taught them."* (John 8:1 Message)

You're listening to Jesus' teaching when suddenly you are interrupted. A group of the religious leaders have caught a woman who has broken one of the religious laws – one of the Top 10. She has committed adultery.

*"Teacher, this woman was caught red-handed in the act of adultery. Moses, in the Law, gives orders to stone such persons. What do you say?"* (John 8:4-5 Message)

This is the perfect trap. Is Jesus going to give her the death penalty or compromise the law by letting her go free? What is Jesus going to do? What is he going to say? She's trembling. They're mad. You're nervous. Jesus is calm.

He bends down and begins writing with his finger in the dirt. What is he writing? Why is he writing? And then he says it: *"The sinless one among you, go first: Throw the stone."* (John 8:7 Message)

Jesus does not let her go nor does he give her the death penalty. He gives the person who is perfect and without sin the permission to carry out the punishment. You're wondering who is going to throw the first stone.

And what happens next is amazing but not surprising – not now. You hear something. Thud. Your head turns. One person drops their stone to the ground and walks away. Then another. Thud. One by one the stones drop out of their hands. Thud. They hit the ground. Thud. Until all of the religious leaders are gone.

Here you are with a front row seat as Jesus turns to the guilty woman and says: *"Where are your accusers? Didn't even one of them condemn you? ... Neither do I. Go and sin no more."* (John 8:10-11 NLT)

And with that, Jesus gives her grace. She hasn't asked for it. She hasn't done anything to deserve it. And neither have you.

What if she goes back to her sinful lifestyle? What if she doesn't change? You don't know for sure. But you do know that by being there your heart has changed.

She doesn't realize that although he is letting her go here, he will be taking her place of punishment later...on the cross. And neither do you...yet. You will. So will the rest of the world.

At some point in life, we all find ourselves either holding stones to throw in judgment or on the ground guilty of not doing what is right. Most of the time...it's both. And Jesus changes us with aggressive grace.

## The Big Idea:
Jesus changes people with aggressive grace.

## Question:
What does aggressive grace look like to you?

## Think about Jesus' words
*"The sinless one among you, go first; Throw the stone."*
*John 8:7 (Message)*

## Day 32
# People do amazing things when they get grace

### Jesus' grace surprises Zacchaeus

*Zacchaeus just stood there, a little stunned. He stammered apologetically, "Master, I give away half my income to the poor — and if I'm caught cheating, I pay four times the damages."*
*Luke 19:8 (Message)*

People do amazing things when they get grace. In fact, people do more from getting grace than the religious leaders demand from the Law. These people become the unlikely Jesus apprentices who do amazing things for God on the mission. These are the people who change the world.

So how does Jesus do this?

Jesus changes what you care about. Jesus' first priority isn't to change what you do. It's not even to change what you believe. It's to change what you care about. While the Kingdom of Rome cares about power and pleasures and the Kingdom of Religion cares about the rules, Jesus cares about the heart.

Jesus said, *"...first clean the inside of the cup and dish, and then the outside also will be clean." (Matthew 23:26 NIV)*

Jesus gets the heart right first. Why? Because if you get the heart right, the rest will follow. And people with changed hearts, change the world. Power brokers can't change the world because you can't force people to change...at least they won't stay that way. Pleasure seekers and rule keepers have nothing to change the hearts of people. And they don't inspire anybody to do anything amazing.

The Kingdom of God causes people to do amazing things because they "get grace." Jesus gives grace to people that the religious leaders would never accept. And these people who get grace do things that the religious leaders would never ask for.

On the mission with Jesus, you come into a city called Jericho. Everyone in the town has turned out to see this Jesus. And it must feel pretty good to be walking with Jesus absorbing the applause of the fans. People are everywhere. There is barely enough room for you and the other apprentices.

Suddenly, Jesus stops and looks up into a tree and sees a man there.

*"When Jesus got to the tree, he looked up and said, 'Zacchaeus, hurry down. Today is my day to be a guest in your home.'" (Luke 19:5 Message)*

Jesus invites himself into Zacchaeus' life. By going to Zacchaeus' house, Jesus accepts him. And this bothers people because Zacchaeus is a tax collector. This is the last person that they think should get grace.

*"Everyone who saw the incident was indignant and grumped, 'What business does he have getting cozy with this crook?'" (Luke 19:7 Message)*

Aggressive grace bothers people – especially people who have worked hard to get all the outside stuff right. In their mind, Zacchaeus hasn't paid his dues. He doesn't deserve grace.

Aggressive grace stuns the people in the culture who get it. And aggressive grace will stun you. Because you know and the people in the culture know you don't deserve it either.

*"Zacchaeus just stood there a little bit stunned." (Luke 19:8 Message)*

And then Zacchaeus does something amazing – something more than the religious leaders would dare ask.

*"He stammered apologetically, 'Master, I give away half of my income to the poor – and if I am caught cheating, I pay back four times the damages." (Luke 19:8 Message)*

Aggressive grace causes people to give more and do more than the religious leaders would ever demand. Why? Because people who get grace give from their hearts. And people who give from their hearts, give in amazing ways. They give what they know they will miss.

Pleasure seekers don't do amazing things. Religious rules don't inspire people to do amazing things. Grace does. The people who get grace love the most. And those who don't get it love the least.

Jesus put it this way, *"…but a person who is forgiven little shows only little love." Luke 7:47 (NLT)*

People do amazing things when they get grace.

## The Big Idea:
People do amazing things when they get grace.

## Question:
What amazing things have you seen
people do who got grace?

## Think about Jesus' words
*I tell you, her sins—and they are many—have been forgiven, so
she has shown me much love. But a person who is forgiven little
shows only little love." Luke 7:47 (NLT)*

## Day 33
# People problems are the huge problems

### Jesus teaches his apprentices about forgiveness

*Then Peter came to him and asked, "Lord, how often should I forgive someone who sins against me? Seven times?" "No, not seven times, Jesus replied, "but seventy times seven!"*
*Matthew 18:21-22 (NLT)*

People problems are the huge problems. But when you think about the huge problems of the world, what comes to your mind? Natural disasters, disease, catastrophes, war … what else? These are huge problems. But why? Because they affect people.

People problems are the biggest problems in the world because of the tremendous value that God places on people. People matter to God.

People problems are the hardest to deal with. Other problems may be unavoidable or incurable. But people problems can usually be avoided or healed. People problems need grace. That is why Jesus' plan to change the world is by changing people's hearts with grace.

But where do you draw the line of grace? That is what Jesus' apprentices wanted to know. How far is too far with this aggressive grace stuff?

*Then Peter came to him and asked, "Lord, how often should I forgive someone who sins against me? Seven times?" "No, not seven times,*

*Jesus replied, "but seventy times seven!" Matthew 18:21-22 (NLT)*

Jesus answers the question with a story to teach his apprentices what forgiveness is and what it is not, and how grace works in the Kingdom of God.

Imagine that you owe a debt (maybe this isn't hard for you). This debt is something that no matter how hard and how long you work, you will never be able to pay it off. (Sound familiar???)

*"…He couldn't pay up, so the King ordered the man, along with his wife, children, and goods to be auctioned off at the slave market." (Matthew 18:25 Message)*

Can you imagine that? You and your loved ones being auctioned off to pay for a debt you owe? What would you do? Here's what the man in the story did: *"The poor wretch threw himself at the king's feet and begged, "Give me a chance and I'll pay it all back." Touched by his pleas, the king let him off, erasing the debt." (Matthew 18:26-27 Message)*

Jesus teaches you that grace is not something you can work for. The king forgives your debt. He doesn't forget it. He erases it.

How awesome would that be! You would be so happy. It would be like the best day ever! And you would never forget that. And neither does the king, because forgiveness does not mean forgetting – it means no longer counting the debt against them. Forgiveness is not cheap. It costs the king a lot.

So how would you respond? You would probably be in a good mood. So, would you turn around and forgive people who owe you? Of course, right? Well, this man didn't.

*"The servant was no sooner out of the room when he came upon one of his fellow servants who owed him ten dollars. He seized him by the throat and demanded, "Pay up. Now!" (Matthew 18:28 Message)*

Why did he act this way? Probably because he didn't really get grace. It was given to him, but he didn't get it. And because he didn't get it, he didn't give it. Grace is something that once you really get; it has to get inside of you so you can give it to others.

So, what happens next? The king finds out and has the man arrested.

*"The king was furious and put the screws to the man until he paid back his entire debt. And that's exactly what my Father in heaven is going to do to each one of you who doesn't forgive unconditionally anyone who asks for mercy." (Matthew 18:34-35 Message)*

Do you think at this point the man wished that he hadn't made a big deal over ten bucks? Absolutely. So then, is that what it is like for you when you don't forgive others? What are you waiting for to give someone grace?

Jesus said: *"If you enter your place of worship and, about to make an offering, you suddenly remember a grudge a friend has against you, abandon your offering, leave immediately, go to this friend and make things right." (Matthew 5:23-24 Message)*

Leave immediately…go…make things right. It's far easier to think that you've made things right because you talked to God about it. But you haven't made it right until you talk to the other person. How do you do it?

First you get your heart right. How do you know when your heart is right? Your heart is right when you're ready to listen to them, you're willing to let Jesus have the last word, and your desire is for your relationship to get closer.

Jesus said: *"If another believer sins against you, go privately and point out the offense. If the other person listens and confesses it, you have won that person back. (Matthew 18:15 NLT)*

Face-to-face you give the same grace that God has given you. Maybe the other person will change, maybe they won't. But you will. Imagine if everyone in the world lived out Jesus' prayer for his apprentices: *"And forgive us our sins, as we have forgiven those who sin against us." (Matthew 6:12 NLT)*

The reason why Jesus can change the world by changing people's hearts is because people problems really are the huge problems of the world. All the other problems are minor in comparison, because God made us to last forever. And that is exactly why we need aggressive grace.

## The Big Idea:
People problems are huge problems.

## Question:
What is keeping you from giving someone grace?

## Think about Jesus' words
*"Forgive us our debts as we have also forgiven our debtors."*
*Matthew 6:12 (NIV)*

## Day 34
# You can't do it yourself

### The vines and the branches

*"Yes, I am the vine; you are the branches. Those who remain in me, and I in them, will produce much fruit. For apart from me you can do nothing." John 15:5 (NLT)*

You can't do it yourself. There are a lot of things that you can change. But you can't change you. Only God can. You can change your mind, you can change your appearance, and you can even change your habits. But it takes God to change your heart.

Every year, especially right around the beginning of the year, people make promises to themselves to make changes in their life. For many people the resolution they make is to exercise and eat better so that their body somewhat resembles something they hope for in their head.

They buy new clothes and a new membership at the gym to start a new fitness plan. And depending on how well they train and how much support they get, they change.

But what really changes? People's hearts or people's waistlines? And what really stays changed?

Outside changes don't stick unless the inside changes first. And that is exactly how Jesus changes you. Jesus changes your life by working on your heart. You work out into your life what Jesus works into your heart. You can't do it yourself. You do it with him.

*"Live in me. Make your home in me just as I do in you." (John 15:4 Message)*

*You can't do it yourself.* Jesus is your source of Life. Jesus invites you into his life. You live in him, and he lives in you as you go on this mission. You remain together.

*"I am the real vine...live in me...you can't bear fruit unless you are joined with me." (John 15:1,4 Message)*

Remain in the grace that got you started with Jesus. That is the grace that will continue to shape your heart like him. As you remain in him, Jesus works into your heart things that eventually everyone gets to see. Stuff that shows you're on the mission. Stuff that shows you really care about people. The most powerful thing that people see in your new life is love.

*You can't do it yourself.* God continues to work on your heart after you've said yes to following Jesus.

*"...my Father is the Farmer. He cuts off every branch of me that doesn't bear grapes. And every branch that is grape-bearing he prunes back so it will bear even more ..." (John 15:1-3 Message)*

How does God work in you? One of the things that God does is cut off everything that is dead. Now that your heart has been changed, Jesus will begin to speak to you about things in your life that must be cut off.

In the Kingdom of Religion, you cut off the people in the culture. In the Kingdom of Rome, you don't cut off anything. Neither of these ways change the world, because they don't change your heart.

Jesus will begin to speak to you about heart issues like

jealousy, pride, lust, hate, etc. What you'll notice is that when you cut out some of these heart issues, it may change some of the things you do – not because of some religious rules but because of a love relationship.

Are there some things that Jesus is speaking to you about cutting out of your life?

Not only does God cut off, but He also cuts back. Jesus will speak to you about things that have your heart that aren't necessarily bad, they're just in the way of you growing and making a bigger difference in the world. What are you doing that takes so much of yourself that it takes you away from the mission?

The bottom line is you only have so much time and energy and resources. What are you going to give your life to?

*You can't do it yourself.* God will continue to work in your heart until every area of your life has been changed by his grace…or until you die.

*"This is how my Father shows who he is – when you produce grapes, when you mature as my disciples." (John 15:8 Message)*

You can't do it yourself…and you don't have to.

## The Big Idea:
You can't do it yourself.

## Question:
What are some areas where God's grace is still changing you?

## Think about Jesus' words
*"Yes, I am the vine; you are the branches. Those who remain in me, and I in them, will produce much fruit. For apart from me you can do nothing. John 15:5 (NLT)*

## Day 35

# One huge act of grace

### Jesus' teaching on responding with grace

*"… If anyone slaps you on the right cheek, turn to him the other also…if anyone forces you to go one mile, go with him two miles."* Matthew 5:39-40 (ESV)

Huge acts of grace change the world. Sounds powerful, huh. Powerful…as long as you're not the one who has to give it. Grace may be free, but it's not cheap. Grace hurts. It just doesn't hurt the other person. When you give people grace, it hurts you because it costs you something. Just like it cost Jesus to give you grace. It hurts and it's worth it.

Huge acts of grace are needed when there are huge problems and huge offenses. If they weren't huge, you could overlook them. But the huge problems of the world cannot be overlooked. People need grace. Aggressive grace is needed most when it is hardest to give.

Jesus teaches his apprentices to give grace to people who want to hurt them.

*"Here's another old saying that deserves a second look: 'Eye for eye, tooth for tooth.' Is that going to get us anywhere? Here's what I propose: 'Don't hit back at all.' If someone strikes you, stand there and take it."* (Matthew 5:38-39 Message)

So how do you respond when people hurt you? What did Jesus do? Jesus chose not to hit back. On the way to the cross he absorbed the punishment—and offered forgiveness instead. Jesus shows you how to love, bless, forgive and pray for the people who hurt you. It's aggressive grace. Not exactly what you want to do to people who hit you. But it's the test of the Jesus apprentice.

Jesus said, *"... love your enemies! Do good to those who hate you. (Luke 6:27 NLT)*

The biggest act of grace ever was the cross. Jesus' mission to change the world by changing people's hearts did not lead him to a throne in Rome but to a Roman cross. Somehow Jesus' death and resurrection changes the world.

Here is the one huge act of grace that changed the world taken from Luke's Gospel:

*Leaving there, he went, as he so often did, to Mount Olives. The disciples followed him. When they arrived at the place, he said, "pray that you don't give into temptation."*

*He pulled away from them about a stone's throw, knelt down, and prayed, "Father, remove this cup from me. But please, not what I want. What do you want?" At once an angel from heaven was at his side, strengthening him. He prayed on all the harder. Sweat, wrung from him like drops of blood, poured off his face.*

*He got up from prayer, went back to the disciples and found them asleep, drugged by grief. He said, "What business do you have sleeping? Get up. Pray so you won't give in to temptation."*

*No sooner were the words out of his mouth than a crowd showed up, Judas, the one from the Twelve, in the lead. He came right up to Jesus to kiss him. Jesus said, "Judas, you would betray the Son of Man with a kiss?"*

*When those with him saw what was happening, they said, "Master, shall we fight?" One of them took a swing at the Chief Priest's servant and cut off his right ear.*

*Jesus said, "Let them be. Even in this." Then, touching the servant's ear, he healed him.*

*Jesus spoke to those who had come — high priests, Temple police, religion leaders: "What is this, jumping me with swords and clubs as if I were a dangerous criminal? Day after day I've been with you in the Temple and you've not so much as lifted a hand against me. But do it your way — it's a dark night, a dark hour.*

*Arresting Jesus, they marched him off and took him into the house of the Chief Priest...The men in charge of Jesus began poking fun at him, slapping him around. They put a blindfold on him and taunted, "Who hit you that time?" ...*

*Then they took Jesus to Pilate...Pilate called in the high priests, rulers, and the others and said, "You brought this man to me as a disturber of the peace. ...it's clear that he's done nothing wrong, let alone anything deserving death. I'm going to warn him to watch his step and let him go."*

*At that, the crowd went wild: "Kill him! ...Crucify! Crucify Him!" ... Pilate caved in and gave them what they wanted. He released the man throw in prison for rioting and murder and gave them Jesus to do whatever they wanted.*

*As they led him off, they made Simon, a man from Cyrene who happened to be coming in from the countryside, carry the cross behind Jesus. A huge crowd of people followed, along with women weeping and carrying on...*

*Two others, both criminals, were taken along with him for execution. When they got to the place called Skull Hill, they crucified him, along with the criminals, one on his right, the other on his left.*

*Jesus prayed, "Father, forgiven them: they don't' know what they're doing."*

*Dividing up his clothes, they threw dice for them. The people stood there staring at Jesus, and the ringleaders made faces, taunting, "He saved others. Let's see him save himself! The Messiah of God – ha! The Chosen – ha!*

*The soldiers also came up and poked fun at him, making a game of it. They toasted him with sour wine: "So you're King of the Jews! Save yourself!" Printed over him was a sign: THIS IS THE KING OF THE JEWS!*

*One of the criminals hanging alongside cursed him: "Some Messiah you are! Save yourself! Save us!" But the other one made him shut up: "Have you no fear of God? You're getting the same as him. We deserve this, but not him – he did nothing to deserve this." Then he said, "Jesus, remember me when you enter your kingdom." He said, 'Don't worry, I will. Today you will join me in paradise."*

*By now it was noon. The whole earth became dark, the darkness lasting three hours – a total blackout. The Temple curtain split right down the middle. Jesus called loudly, "Father, I place my life in your hands!" Then he breathed his last...*

*At the crack of dawn on Sunday, the women came to the tomb...they found the entrance stone rolled back from the tomb, so they walked in. But once inside, they couldn't find the body of the Master Jesus.*

*Then, out of nowhere it seemed, two men, light cascading over them, stood there..." Why are you looking for the Living One in a cemetery? He is not here, but raised up." ...*

*...the Eleven and their friends gathered together, talking away: "It's really happened! The Master has been raised up...while they were saying all this, Jesus appeared to them and said, "Peace be with you." They thought they were seeing a ghost and were scared half to death...look at my hands, look at my feet – it's really me. Touch me...*

*Then he said, "Everything I told you while I was with you comes to this…you can see now how it is written that the Messiah suffers, rises from the dead on the third day, and then a total life-change through the forgiveness of sins is proclaimed in his name to all nations…*(Excerpts from Luke 22-23 Message).

On the cross with nails in his hands and feet – with a crown of thorns on his head, Jesus gives the world aggressive grace.

*"Father, forgive them, for they don't know what they are doing…" (Luke 23:34 NLT)*

How could you hear that and not be changed? How could anyone?

The cross is the place where God forgives people without lowering his standards.

*"God sent his Son into the world not to judge the world, but to save the world through him." (John 3:17 NLT)*

Grace doesn't let people off the hook. Grace takes people's place on the hook for them. Grace changes the world because grace changes people's hearts. Jesus died for you, for your sins, to change your heart. It's grace…and it changes the world.

## The Big Idea:
Jesus gave us one huge act of grace.

## Question:
How does Jesus' huge act of grace on the cross change your heart?

## Think about Jesus' words
*"Father, forgive them, for they do not know what they are doing." Luke 23:34 (NLT)*

## Week Eight
# Practice #7:
# Jesus apprentices make more apprentices

## The Great Commission

*Therefore go and make disciples of all nations, baptizing them in the name of the Father and the Son and the Holy Spirit. Teach these new disciples to obey all the commands I have given you. And be sure of this: I am with you always, even to the end of the age. Matthew 28:19-20 (NLT)*

# Introduction
# Week Eight

Jesus did some amazing things on earth. But he said that his apprentices would do even greater things. How is that possible? He's the one who's God.

But as long as Jesus was on earth, he was limited to one human body. He changed the hearts and lives of all he healed, but he could not humanly get to everyone. If Jesus had remained on earth, he would have become a bottleneck to what he cared most about – changing people's hearts.

So, Jesus poured his life into twelve apprentices to change the world by making more apprentices who would make more apprentices to help heal the world. And when Jesus ascended to the Father, he left his words and sent his spirit to his apprentices.

Now instead of one human Jesus walking around with twelve apprentices, Jesus lives through the lives of millions of apprentices who inspire more apprentices to help heal the world. Do you want to help heal the world? You can. Go on the mission with Jesus and make more apprentices.

## Day 36
# People becoming the church

### Jesus speaking to one of his apprentices

*And now I'm going to tell you who you are, really are. You are Peter- a rock. This is the rock on which I will put together my church, a church so expansive with energy that not even the gates of hell will be able to keep it out.*
*Matthew 16:18 (Message)*

What do you think a church is? Is it a building? An organization? A business? A club? If you were to ask someone, what would they say? Would they say that the church is people? Jesus would.

According to Jesus, the church is people – his apprentices – on a mission together with him to change the world by changing people's hearts.

In the Kingdom of Rome, temples were places where the gods lived. You could visit them. Ask for their help. Make an offering. And hope that the gods heard you.

In the Kingdom of Religion, there was only one true God and he lived in THE temple in Jerusalem. The temple was the place for God's presence.

If you grew up in the kingdom of Religion, you knew the history of God setting your people free from slavery in Egypt and his presence going with you through the desert. The sign of God's presence was a cloud by day and a ball of fire by night.

In the desert, God gave one of your founding fathers, Moses, the instructions to organize the two million Israelites. Each person would live in a tribe (12 total) and in the center of everyone was a portable tent – this tent was called the Tabernacle and was the meeting place for the presence of God.

This tent was the centerpiece of this traveling community and where Moses met with God for direction and blessing. The Tabernacle contained sacred reminders of God's miracles and the Ark of the Covenant that represented his presence. The Tabernacle also became the blueprint for your temple that was planned by one of your kings, David, and finished by his son, King Solomon.

The Temple courts were the center of society, and the Temple was where priests served God. On special holy days and celebrations, people would travel from far and wide to go to the Temple to worship God.

So how different is that from today? Don't people today think that God lives in a building? Isn't it true that on special holidays and celebrations, people visit God at the "church" building?

Jesus came to teach his apprentices that God doesn't live in a building but wants to live in human hearts by inviting us to live in his presence everywhere they went.

It's not that Jesus didn't respect the temple. In fact, he raised the bar of respect when he kicked out those who were using the Temple to make money off of people who came to worship God.

*"Jesus put a whip together out of strips of leather and chased them out*

*of the temple…get your things out of here! Stop turning my Father's house into a shopping mall." (John 2:15-16 Message)*

What was Jesus so upset about – the building or people's hearts? I think it was people's hearts. Jesus was angry because these money-makers were creating an environment that made people feel taken advantage of. It turned people off towards God. Does that happen today?

Now listen to what Jesus said next: *"Tear down this temple and in three days I will build it back up." (John 2:19 Message)*

What was Jesus talking about? Do you know? The apprentices didn't…not until after Jesus died and rose again after three days. In their minds, the temple was where God lived.

Jesus was teaching his apprentices that he was God and that he would live inside of everyone who comes into his life. That's the church. Jesus – God's presence – living and moving through His apprentices to change the world. That's the church. *You don't go to church.* You become the church.

The Greek word for church is *ekklesia* and literally means "called out ones". Do you get it? The church is people – the apprentices that Jesus calls out to change the world with Him.

Jesus asked His apprentices who they thought He was. What would you say? One of the apprentices, Peter, said, *"You are the Christ, the Messiah, the Son of the Living God." (Matthew 16:16 Message)*

Then Jesus says this about Peter: *"And now I am going to tell you who you are, really are. You are Peter, a rock. This is the rock on which I will put together my church, a church so expansive with energy that not even the gates of hell will be able to keep it out." (Matthew*

*16:18 Message)*

Do you see it now? Who you think Jesus is directly affects what you think about the church. If you think that Jesus is a great religious teacher, then the church might as well be a building because he's going to need some place to teach. But if you believe Jesus is the Messiah – Savior of the World, then the church is his people empowered by his spirit to change the world. The church is people on the mission with Jesus.

You don't go to church. You don't have church. You don't even invite people to church. You become the church. You go on a mission as the church. You gather as the church. You worship with others who are the church. And you invite people to participate in the life of the church.

The church as a building will never change the world because hearts don't stay changed by visiting God – whether weekly or once a year. The only way people's hearts really change is when they live in God's presence twenty-four hours a day, seven days a week. That's the church that changes the world.

People becoming the church are the apprentices that Jesus uses to do even greater things than he did on earth. Because instead of Jesus healing people and changes hearts through one human body, Jesus is alive through his Church – millions of people on the mission to change the world with him.

And not even hell can stop that.

## The Big Idea:
The church is not a building – it's people on a mission with Jesus.

## Question:
What group of apprentices are you becoming the church with?

## Think about Jesus' words
*"… I will put together my church, a church so expansive with energy that not even the gates of hell will be able to keep it out. Matthew 16:18 (Message)*

## Day 37
# The church shows the world the good life

### The picture of the early church

*...and all the believers lived in wonderful harmony, holding everything in common. They sold whatever they owned and pooled their resources so that each person's need was met...*
*Acts 2:43-45 (Message)*

The church shows the world the good life. What it looks like to live together in the Kingdom of God. The church should be humanity at its best. But is that what people think? Is that what you think? When you think of the church do you think of what could be or shouldn't be?

One of the reasons why it's easy to see flaws in the church is because people are in it. It's people becoming the church. It's a process. The church is full of imperfect people being changed from the inside out. And that means you can't always see the changes that have already started in the heart and are working their way out.

Churches are not perfect. Look at the nine books in the New Testament that are letters written to churches and seven letters just in one book (Revelation) written to churches – there is no perfect church. At least not yet. God is still at work bringing his Kingdom into this world.

But does the world need a church that looks perfect on the outside or an imperfect church that is in the process of being changed? What do you want? What inspires you more? A human being who doesn't seem real or a real person who seems very human but is changing right before your eyes.

The early church was changing right in front of the culture. The early church stuck out. This group of people on the mission with Jesus loved each other so much, so deeply that they showed the world the good life. They lived out the Kingdom of God. Not perfectly, but sincerely. This was Jesus' prayer for them and for the church today.

On the night Jesus was betrayed and arrested, he prayed this in the Garden: *"I am praying not only for these disciples, but also for all who will ever believe in me through their message … I pray that they will all be one, just as you and I are one – as you are in me, Father, and I am in you. And may they be in us so that the world will believe you sent me." John 17:20-21 (NLT)*

In the same way that best friends and close-knit families love each other, this group of people cared for one another. They lived out what the world wanted: harmony.

*"… And all the believers lived in wonderful harmony, holding everything in common. They sold whatever they owned and pooled their resources so that each person's need was met…" (Acts 2:43-45 Message)*

What if you could be a part of a church like that? Do you think that Jesus would use a church like that in the 21st century to change people's hearts?

Look at what they did. They made sure that everyone's need was met. Can you imagine that? Isn't that what all of us want? Isn't that what you want? Perhaps you would do that for your family… But maybe that is the point. They treated each other like real family.

This real family gathered together to worship. This real family prayed for each other. This real family ate meals together. This real family celebrated and did life together. And this real family grew in their understanding of Jesus together.

The way they loved each other made people in the culture want to be on the mission, too.

*"People in general liked what they saw. Every day their numbers grew as God added those who were saved." (Acts 2:47 Message)*

This church changed their world. God worked miracles through them. And you have to wonder what God could do with a group of people becoming the church today? Wouldn't it be fun to find out?

## The Big Idea:

The church shows the world the good life.

## Question:

What is Jesus saying to your church?

## Think about Jesus' words

*I pray that they will all be one, just as you and I are one—as you are in me, Father, and I am in you. And may they be in us so that the world will believe you sent me.*
*John 17:21 (NLT)*

## Day 38
# Have you baptized anyone lately?

### Jesus tells His apprentices to baptize

*Go out and train everyone you meet, far and near, in this way of life, marking them by baptism... Matthew 28:19 (Message)*

Have you baptized anyone lately? You can. In fact, according to Jesus if you are one of his apprentices you will. Jesus apprentices baptize more apprentices. Now imagine what that would look like. What if everyone who called themselves a follower of Jesus, baptized people whose hearts had changed and wanted to go on the mission too? Do you think that might make a difference in the world?

Now maybe you've never thought of yourself as someone who baptizes people. Isn't that a job for people who are professionals at the religious stuff? Maybe in your mind, it's like asking someone who is not a pilot to land a plane. But that's not what Jesus said.

When Jesus rose from the dead, he met with his apprentices and gave them this instruction which is known as the Great Commission: *"Go out and train everyone you meet, far and near, in this way of life, marking them by baptism in the threefold name: Father, Son, and Holy Spirit. Then instruct them in the practice of all that I have commanded you. I'll be with you as you do this, day after day after day, right up to the end of the age." Matthew 28:19-20 (Message)*

Do you think it was Jesus' plan that the only people who

would train the world in the Kingdom of God life would be professionals? Doesn't it seem like Jesus thinks that all of his apprentices are going to train more apprentices? And doesn't it seem like Jesus thinks all of his apprentices are going to baptize these new apprentices?

Jesus ties together the baptism and the training. Jesus empowers all of his apprentices to baptize and train so that the mission is not limited to the ability of a few people.

Think about how this changes you. It isn't just professionals doing all the spiritual work, you're in on it. Can you see why having professionals baptize people in a building once a month won't change the world? It won't even change you.

When you baptize someone, they are changed and so are you. The connection that you two already have provides a natural way for both of you to actually obey Jesus' command: apprentice the people you baptize.

You may not think that you're qualified enough to baptize. Like if you were more spiritual… But that's not it. You aren't baptizing them in your name. You're baptizing apprentices in the name of God – the Father, the Son, and the Holy Spirit.

Even before he died on the cross, Jesus had his apprentices baptizing people to go on the mission.

*"…though Jesus himself didn't baptize them – his disciples did…"* (John 4:2 NLT)

Jesus' plan to change the world by changing people's hearts includes all of his apprentices baptizing.

Look, there are only two practices that Jesus told his apprentices to keep doing: one was baptism and the other was communion. Both of these remind his apprentices about his death and resurrection and the mission to change the world by changing people's hearts. Both of these have somehow become 21st century examples of how Jesus' apprentices don't own the mission – only the professionals do.

Baptism is powerful. Both for the person being baptized and the one baptizing. Jesus modeled baptism for his apprentices by being baptized himself.

*"At this time, Jesus came from Nazareth in Galilee and was baptized by John in the Jordan." (Mark 1:9 Message)*

Jesus was baptized before he launched his public "Change the World Tour" and before he was tempted for forty days in the desert. Jesus' baptism was a significant moment in his life where he got to hear his Father's approval.

*"You are my Son, chosen and marked by my love, pride of my life." (Mark 1:11 Message)*

God's approval is something that all Jesus apprentices experience when they are baptized. When you are baptized you know at that moment that God is pleased with you.

The early apprentices begin baptizing people into this "Change the World Movement" after Peter gives his message on the day of Pentecost:

*"… Change your life. Turn to God and be baptized, each of you, in the name of Jesus Christ, so your sins are forgiven…That day about three thousand took him at his word, were baptized and were signed up." Acts 2:38, 41 (Message)*

Have you been baptized in water as a believer? You can sign up today. If you want to go on the mission with Jesus, the way you let everyone in your life know is you get baptized in water. If you haven't, why not do it now.

Is there someone, a Jesus apprentice, that God has used to change your heart? Why don't you ask them today if they will baptize you? Invite your friends and family to participate and find some water. It will be a great celebration. And who knows... maybe one of your friends or family members will want you to baptize them, too.

## The Big Idea:
Have you baptized anyone lately?

## Question:
What is keeping you from baptizing someone or being baptized?

## Think about Jesus' words
*"Therefore go and make disciples of all nations baptizing them in the name of the Father and of the Son and of the Holy Spirit, and teaching them to obey everything I have commanded you. And surely I will be with you always, to the very end of the age." Matthew 28:19-20 (NLT)*

## Day 39
# It's all about Jesus

### Jesus' power to His apprentices

*But you will receive power when the Holy Spirit comes upon you. And you will be my witnesses, telling people about me everywhere – in Jerusalem, throughout Judea, in Samaria, and to the ends of the earth.* Acts 1:8 (NLT)

It's all about Jesus. There are a lot of things in life that will not make sense unless you look at them through the lens of Jesus and his mission. There's a lot in the Bible that may not make any sense to you unless you read it through the story of Jesus and His mission.

All of the Old Testament laws, history, poetry, and prophets point to Jesus and only make sense in light of his mission. You can find yourself practicing rituals that were never written for you if you don't read them through Jesus' mission.

All of the New Testament letters and the end time events only make sense when read through the person and mission of Jesus. If you don't understand this, you may end up with some strange theology.

It's all about Jesus. Jesus teaches his apprentices to look at the Bible and life through his mission to change the world by changing people's hearts.

*"He went on to open their understanding of the Word of God, showing them how to read their Bibles this way. He said, "You can see now how it is written that the Messiah suffers, rises from the dead on the*

*third day, and then a total life-change through the forgiveness of sins is proclaimed in his name to all nations – starting here…" (Luke 24:45-47 Message)*

It's all about Jesus, and when you're all about Jesus, you get all of Jesus' power. That's probably hard to believe because Jesus had so much power to change lives. But Jesus is the one who gives it to you, not me. Jesus gives you his power by sending his Spirit into your life so you can to live out his Kingdom.

The same power that Jesus had on earth is the same power that he gave to the early apprentices and the same power that he offers you. But here's what is important. Jesus' power is only for the mission – his mission and not yours. It's all about Jesus.

His power is for his mission. The early apprentices struggled with this so it's probably no surprise that people still do today.

After Jesus rose from the dead, he met with His apprentices over forty days.

*"He presented himself alive to them in many different settings…in face-to-face meetings, he talked to them about things concerning the Kingdom of God." (Acts 1:3 Message)*

Can you imagine being one of the apprentices at this point? Talk about a rollercoaster ride. In a short time, you've gone from thinking that you and Jesus are going to change the world…to Jesus is dead and it's was all just a bad dream. To now, Jesus is alive again – let's dominate the world.

At this point, you've got to be thinking, "Wow…what an incredible plan!" Ingenious…now that Jesus has conquered death, let's conquer the Kingdom of Rome." That's what the Jesus apprentices were thinking.

*"Master, are you going to restore the kingdom to Israel? Is this the time?" (Acts 1:6 Message)*

The apprentices were still seeing things through the lens of self. It's like saying, "Hey Jesus, here's how you could use your power that would really be cool for me."

But Jesus' power is for the mission to change the world by changing hearts not to make your life better. Weird things happen when people try to use Jesus power for their own benefit. Ever seen it?

Jesus' power is for his mission. The power is for one thing: to point people to Jesus.

*"But you will receive power when the Holy Spirit comes upon you. And you will be my witnesses, telling people about me everywhere – in Jerusalem, throughout Judea, in Samaria, and to the ends of the earth." (Acts 1:8 NLT)*

Jesus apprentices are Jesus' witnesses to the culture. As an apprentice, you show the culture the good life – the Kingdom of God, and he gives you the power to do it.

Where do you start? Jerusalem…start right where you are. Who are the people who are already in your life that you already have relationship with that are not yet on the mission with Jesus? You know them, they know you. You speak their language. They know your heart. That is your Jerusalem.

Where else do you go? Judea and Samaria…to those who are nearby but different. You know them, but you're not like them. They are not like you, but they know you. You will need to connect with them in their world before they will listen. You will probably have to listen first. That is your Judea and Samaria.

So then, what is the ends of the earth? How far is that? It is those who are not like you and don't know you. They are far from you although they may be closer to God than you think. You will need to learn from them before they will learn from you. That is your ends of the earth.

What if they don't believe what you say? Jesus promises to go with you and provide proof for the message.

*"And the disciples went everywhere preaching, the Master working right with them, validating the Message with indisputable evidence." (Mark 16:20 Message)*

It's all about Jesus. And when it's all about Jesus, Jesus does powerful things – the supernatural – miracles. That is what the early apprentices experienced. And that is what he wants you to experience, too.

## The Big Idea:
It's all about Jesus.

## Question:
How does Jesus and his mission affect how you look at some of your life experiences?

## Think about Jesus' words
*"But you will receive power when the Holy Spirit comes upon you. And you will be my witnesses, telling people about me everywhere…" Acts 1:8 (NLT)*

## Day 40
# Have you started a church today?

### Jesus describes how His Kingdom grows

*Here is another illustration Jesus used: "The kingdom of heaven is like a mustard seed ... it is the smallest of all seeds, but it becomes the largest of garden plants; it grows into a tree, and birds comes and make nests in its branches.*
*Matthew 13:31-32 (NLT)*

Have you started a church today? If you think that a church is a building, probably not. But if a church is people on the mission with Jesus, then maybe you have.

Inside of every follower of Jesus is the seed of a church, because every apprentice has the potential to make more apprentices. And every apprentice has the potential to change someone's heart. This is how God's Kingdom spreads through people. It starts in your heart, changes you, and then spreads to someone else and changes them.

Jesus told a number of stories about the Kingdom of God and how it grows and changes the world by changing hearts.

In one story, a farmer plants seed that lands on four different types of soil. The seed is the message of grace and the soil represents our hearts.

One seed lands on the road and is stolen. This is like the person who hears the message of grace and doesn't respond.

*"...the Evil One comes along and plucks it right out of that person's heart. This is the seed the farmer scatters on the road." (Matthew 13:19 Message)*

Another seed lands on the gravel. It starts to grow but doesn't last. This is like the apprentice who starts to follow but quits when it gets tough.

*"The person who hears and instantly responds with enthusiasm. But there is no soil of character, and so when the emotions wear off and some difficulty arrives, there is nothing to show for it. (Matthew 13:20-21 Message)*

A third seed lands in the weeds and gets choked out like the apprentice who gets sidetracked.

*"...But weeds of worry and illusions about getting more and wanting everything under the sun strangle what was heard, and nothing comes of it." (Matthew 13:22 Message)*

The final seed lands on the good soil and produces a ton of fruit. This is like the apprentice whose changed heart changes the world.

*"The seed cast on good earth is the person who hears and takes in the News, and then produces a harvest beyond his wildest dreams." (Matthew 13:23 Message)*

Jesus teaches you that the number one key to his church growing is your heart. God's Kingdom starts small and grows large through changed hearts. Jesus calls these changed hearts mustard seeds.

*"The kingdom of heaven is like a mustard seed ... it is the smallest of all seeds, but it becomes the largest of garden plants; it grows into a tree, and birds come and make nests in its branches." Matthew 13:31-32 (NLT)*

God's Kingdom is genetically programed to grow! The only thing you can do to slow it down is to keep it from growing inside of you. The most important thing you do as an apprentice is keep your heart right. When your heart is right, God's Kingdom grows inside of you. And when God's Kingdom grows inside of you, more people become apprentices.

*Every day their number grew as God added those who were saved. Acts 2:47 (Message)*

Who knows…maybe you have started a church today.

## The Big Idea:
Have you started a church today?

## Question:
If you could do anything for God what would it be?

## Think about Jesus' words
*"The seed cast on good earth is the person who hears and takes in the News, and then produces a harvest beyond his wildest dreams." Matthew 13:23 (Message)*

# Jesus Apprentice Commitment

- Study the words of Jesus for 40 days by reading the *Jesus Apprentice* book.
- Meet with a Jesus Apprentice group (who are you on the mission with?)
- Look for opportunities to serve people around you with "small acts of grace."

## My apprentice group includes:

_____

_____

_____

_____

_____

_____

_____

# Jesus' 7 practices that help heal the world

1. Jesus invites us into his Life.

2. Jesus shows us his world.

3. Jesus lives in the culture.

4. Jesus apprentices serve the world.

5. Jesus asks for everything.

6. Jesus changes people from the inside out.

7. Jesus apprentices make more apprentices.